D1120404

Reverend J Aelwyn Roberts was Vicar of Llandegai in North Wales for 36 years. As Director of Social Work for the Diocese of Bangor, he found himself increasingly called upon to deal with hauntings and other aspects of the paranormal, which he recounted in his previous book, *Holy Ghostbuster*. A consummate storyteller, he has written many stories and scripts for BBC Radio. He is also a popular broadcaster on Welsh radio and television, and has appeared on radio and television in both the UK and the USA.

by the same author

Holy Ghostbuster

Yesterday's People

—

A PARSON'S SEARCH
FOR HIS NIRVANA

J AELWYN ROBERTS

ELEMENT

Shaftesbury, Dorset • Rockport, Massachusetts
Melbourne, Victoria

© Element Books Limited 1997
Text © Reverend J Aelwyn Roberts 1997

First published in Great Britain in 1997 by
Element Books Limited
Shaftesbury, Dorset SP7 8BP

Published in the USA in 1997 by
Element Books, Inc.
PO Box 830, Rockport, MA 01966

Published in Australia in 1977 by
Element Books
and distributed by Penguin Australia Limited
487 Maroondah Highway, Ringwood, Victoria 3134

All rights reserved.
No part of this book may be reproduced or utilized
in any form or by any means, electronic or mechanical,
without prior permission in writing from the Publisher.

Cover illustration by J Catt
Cover design by Slatter-Anderson
Page design by Roger Lightfoot
Typeset by Bournemouth Colour Press
Printed and bound in Great Britain by Hartnolls Ltd,
Bodmin, Cornwall

British Library Cataloguing in Publication
Data available

Library of Congress Cataloging in Publication
Data available

ISBN 1–86204–000–1

Contents

—

Acknowledgements

——

I am so grateful to my many friends for their help and encouragement; it is their expertise that has made the book possible and not mine. Particularly I would like to thank the following:

Elwyn Roberts, my very good friend and colleague. It was Elwyn who introduced me to most of the 'yesterday's people' I describe in this book. The two of us have also spent many comfortless vigils in haunted places awaiting the pleasure of silly and boring spirits who insisted on playing 'hard to get' on cold and shivering winter's nights.

Chloris Morgan, my wise counsellor, who has taught me so much about this other world about us, and not a little about syntax, and who also (bless her) is acting as proofreader.

Winnie Marshall, who I think still regards me as a mere infant in this other life, sphere or existence she seems to stride in and out of so effortlessly.

The Right Reverend Dr Barry Morgan, the brave and enlightened Bishop of Bangor, who read the manuscript of my book, and instead of instantly unfrocking and excommunicating me, as many another bishop would, chose instead to heap Pauline coals of fire upon my head by agreeing to write the foreword.

Dr Dewi Rees, whose work and researches on bereavement I admire so much, for allowing me to quote so freely from the results of his scholarship.

Element Books, the publishers, who not only produced my book but also adopted me into a family of the most cheerful and efficient book-creating people one can ever find.

John Baldock, my editor – the quiet but knowledgeable man from Element who always managed to get his own way just by being kind and patient.

Bruce Laing, a student who, screwdriver in hand, would descend upon the vicarage whenever my word processor became over-heated and threatened to cease.

It is good to have such friends.

Foreword

—

by the Right Reverend Dr Barry Morgan, Bishop of Bangor

Ask any cleric in the diocese of Bangor about Aelwyn Roberts, and you will be told that he is quite a colourful character. This book and his previous bestseller *Holy Ghostbuster* give ample evidence of his rich and varied ministry. I must confess that I have never experienced ghosts.

Aelwyn, as all who know him might expect, has his own theology. I am not at all sure that he is right about what he says about demons, paradise or the transfiguration, or that he has rightly interpreted various tenets of the Christian faith. Nor am I persuaded that believing in ghosts is proof that there is life with God beyond the grave. Be that as it may, what is obvious to any reader of this book is that Aelwyn was a good and caring parish priest, willing to help anyone in any kind of trouble, full of zest for life and a marvellous storyteller to boot.

The Church of England's Doctrinal Commission has recently published a report, *The Mystery of Salvation*, on salvation which describes judgement not as something God does to us but as something we bring on ourselves in this world and the next through accepting or rejecting God and his love. Judgement is also seen as a process not an event. The Commission's discussions would have been much enlivened had Aelwyn been able to propound his theories about Summerland to it.

† Barry Bangor

1 *The Passing Over*

—

I wonder how many people who enjoy burrowing in bookshops have noticed how the displaying and the shelf-stacking is done. For every single 'Whodunnit' and every single romantic novel sitting on a shelf, there are at least ten DIY books giving careful and explicit instructions on how to carry out a variety of tasks: how to grow roses, how to cook with a wok, and on the top shelves, quite a number on how to make love. There are also whole sections devoted to explaining how to cope with different ailments: how to cope with arthritis, how to cope with migraine, how to cope with an irritable bowel. But a bookshop browser would be very lucky to discover a book on how to cope with dying.

Publishers have been slow to realize that, of the millions of people who walk in and out of the shops where they sell their wares, the nearest thing to a rose garden approximately 75 per cent of them have is a window box, that only 2.25 per cent of them possess a wok, and that the 0.6 per cent of them who suffer the pangs of irritable bowel syndrome manage very well on Fybogel and orange peel and have no need of further instruction. But many publishers seem to ignore the fact that one day all who browse in bookshops – every single one of them – will have to cope with the act of dying, many within the next few months. Yet there is not a DIY book available anywhere that tells them how to do it.

'No, I tell a lie,' as an old parishioner of mine used to say when she got her facts a little mixed up. There *is* a book available on this subject, if only the browser knows what to look out for. It is called *The Tibetan Book of the Dead*, translated by the great scholar Evans-Wentz and published by the Oxford University Press. It describes in great detail the different stages we all have to pass through at death. It teaches us how to look out for different signposts and landmarks as we make the journey, and it even describes the different reactions and emotions we will feel, or ought to feel, as we face new experiences and make new contacts on the way.

Knowledge about the life after this life, and how to get to it, was passed down by word of mouth from generation to generation in Buddhist Tibet until it came to be written in book form in the 8th century. But it is only recently as a result of arduous research and translation by Evans-Wentz that we in the Western world have been able to share in the wisdom and the mysticism of the Buddhist monks of centuries ago. This book tells us that making a good death requires skill, and skill comes from good instruction. And this instruction is found in *The Tibetan Book of the Dead*.

When a person is dying in Tibet a monk is called into the home to instruct him in what to expect in the next stage of existence and how to reach that stage. Even when someone dies suddenly, the monk is called to give instruction. For days he will read into the ear of the dead person the instruction laid down in the book, continuing even during the funeral ceremony. For Buddhists believe that even after death, a person is still able to hear and to understand his 'earth' language for many days. They believe that the last earth faculty to be extinguished is the sense of hearing.

But to parody St Paul's Letter to the Corinthians: 'Some man will say what need is there of a skill to die since death cometh to us all.' The reply to that is: 'Thou fool! Death is not something that cometh to us all. Death is a powerful act each one of us must perform for himself and by himself when the appropriate time comes.'

Doctors, nurses and clergymen who have been present at many deaths would all agree that some do it with grace and dignity, while others make the most awful mess of it. As a clergymen for many years I have seen a lot of people die. Some die peacefully with a smile on their faces and a little sigh. I have seen others squirming in their beds, flailing their arms and with terror in their eyes, clutching at the bedclothes in their efforts to stay in this world. I remember once sitting at the bedside of a dying parishioner who was a wonderful Christian. She was tossing about and in obvious distress. I could not understand it; I would have expected her to have been calm. Then the truth occurred to me and I whispered to her 'Elizabeth and Bryn are on their way. They will be here any time now. I will stay with you until they come'. Immediately there was calmness from the bed. In this case the good Christian mother just could not settle down to practise her well-learned dying skills until she had said goodbye to her grown-up children.What *The Tibetan Book of the Dead* says is true: the dying can hear very clearly what we are saying. Elizabeth and Bryn did arrive in time, but even if they hadn't and their mother had died before they arrived at her bedside, I think I would still have persuaded the two of them have said to her 'Sorry we failed to make it, Mum. We were held up by traffic on the Conwy Bridge.'

At this point the questioner has a right to a second question. I think it would be: 'How can anyone who has not experienced death teach others how to die?' And that is a very good question.

When I was researching this book I asked a friend of mine who is a stalwart Spiritualist about the beliefs of the Spiritualist Church regarding death and the hereafter. She told me: 'We don't have beliefs, we have knowledge.' This knowledge, she told me, is given to them by the spirits of those who have died, and by the spirit guides whose work it is to inform earth-dwellers about death and about the kind of life beyond the grave. I have mingled with these people long enough to realize that this is no idle boast. I have also met many whom I like to think of as yesterday's people, but whom others refer to as ghosts, and I also accept their testimony.

For over 40 years I seem to have been the clergyman in North Wales most often called upon when people are troubled by ghosts. We work as a team really. My friend Elwyn Roberts is a very receptive sensitive. He would not like me to describe him as a medium, because he is also a distinguished member of the Society for Psychical Research, and quite incidentally he is also a crowned bard of the Welsh Gorsedd of Bards. He earns his living as a research physicist. Elwyn Edwards, another crowned bard, is our meticulous diarist and researcher. So here, in this particular corner of North Wales, a parson and two bards can be seen at night visiting homes where human and spirit tenants have difficulty sharing the same kitchen.

Without a shadow of doubt Elwyn has the gift of 'discerning spirits', the gift that according to the New Testament was given to the early Church but was later lost. He has this gift so strongly that if he allowed one to call him through a medium he would have to be further described as a trance-medium – a medium who can enable a spirit to manifest itself to others through him, and by using his body.

I will have to refer to this ghost-helping activity of ours quite often later in the book, so it might be just as well to describe here our rather simple way of working these things out.

The call for help usually comes to me, the parson, by letter or phone, and I decide how urgent it is. Many calls come from people who are just curious to know what causes particular bumps in the night, or who the old lady is who every few months seems to stand on the landing at night watching them as they go to the loo. Curiosity callers such as these are given a five-minute DIY instruction course over the phone; time does not allow for anything else. I usually advise them to speak to the old lady, ask her who she is and how they can help her. There are other people, however, hundreds of them, who are terrified by the activities of ghosts who invade the privacy of their homes without so much as a by your leave. These people are often reluctant to ask for help, as others look pityingly on them when they do. Even ministers of religion often treat those who speak to them of ghosts and poltergeists as half cracked. Those of us who have worked in this part of the Lord's vineyard must never allow bishops and archdeacons to be flippant about such things. People who are troubled very often say that the ghosts not only bump into them in the night, but they also seem to harbour sad and painful memories of things in their earth life that depressed them. These spirits somehow manage to permeate the house with their gloom and depression and make cheerless what, before their arrival, was a happy household. My psychic friends tell me that this is a very well-known fact, and that very often a potential house buyer who is a sensitive has been known to turn down a bargain offer simply because the house did not seem to be a happy one.

So where there is real need for help the team is always prepared to visit. I am the diagnostician. I glean the facts from the householder but I say nothing – not one single word of what I have heard, or any preknowledge I have – to any other member of the party.

The party itself is not too large – just the two Elwyns and me and recently Bridget, my psychologist daughter, who is also interested in ghosts. We also encourage at least some members of the stricken family to sit in with us, as without members of the family present the whole project could turn out to be quite fruitless. It is fear of the unknown, rather than fear of a ghost, that leads people to contact us in the first place. It is this fear of the unknown that drives some of them to consider moving house because of the atmosphere of gloom and despondency they accuse this unknown thing of casting over their lives. So the main exercise is to bring the two parties together. The ghost, 'thing', or 'evil spirit', ceases to be a 'ghost', a 'thing', or 'evil spirit' once it has walked openly into their kitchen and they have all recognized it as just one of yesterday's people – and very often discovered to be a relative of theirs.

We used to work under ordinary house lighting; we accepted without question what was provided. Lately however we have allowed ourselves the little luxury of an infra-red lamp. Elwyn chooses the room we sit in. In fairness to him he usually selects the warmest and most comfortable. He chooses an upright chair for himself and sits with a small table in front of him, on which he places the little infra-red lamp, with its light on his face. The rest of us all take our places just as people do in other people's houses. And we talk; we talk about the family, about how long they have lived in the house, and about their work and their interests. We talk about anything and everything except the ghost we have come to interview. Then after a time, Elwyn will say: 'There is someone here. She is a bit shy and seems a little taken aback at the sight of so many of us in the same room.' Then he speaks again, but not to us: 'No don't go dear. Do stay with us. We're all so pleased to see you, do stay with us.' Then he says something which I always feel requires a tremendous amount of courage: 'Use my body. Enter into my body and use it, if you know how to.'

The rest of us, especially after we introduced the infra-red light, are able to tell whether Elwyn's invitation has been accepted or not – we can actually see his face changing as he takes on the physical appearance of different ghost visitors, some younger, some older than himself. I have seen his features torn with strong emotions as spirits using his body tell horrific tales from the past – like the account of losing three children, all within three months of each other, or the account of witnessing the amputation of a partner's leg in the days before anaesthetic – and his face awash with tears.

After 40 years of finding, talking to and counselling ghosts, the one thing that amazes me is their number. I am always amused when I hear the tale of a so-called exorcist entering a house and saying, 'Yes, there is a presence here. I can feel there is someone here.' Someone indeed! In practically every ghost house our team has visited we have found not just one but a legion of ghosts. I have come to the conclusion that nearly every house in the country has its ghosts and that where there is one, there are many. Frequently we have come across ghosts from different periods and different ages living together under one roof, very often quite amicably, until the new Earth householder begins to complain and call in an exorcist. There is nothing strange about this plurality of spirits of different generations, because yesterday's people are today living in the Eternal Present, where past, present and future are all one. Earth-dwellers need a certain amount of space per person and must think within the limits of time, but space, to the dweller in the spirit world, means nothing.

If it were, as many think, simply a case of going into a house, identifying the errant spirit and cautioning him or her to behave or leave, these visits would not take long. But it is never like that. When Elwyn or some other medium penetrates through whatever it is that they do penetrate, it is not just a case of coming face to face with one particular ghost; it is more like entering Euston Station and having to sift through a great number of passengers before finding the one described by the family. Even after they have been found, they may still decide to be shy or play hard to get on that particular evening. It takes a lot of time to make good contact, and the patience of Job himself. It is very difficult to explain to one's family when one comes in very late after a session that once one has been able to nail down a particular spirit and to get him or her to talk, it is far better to get on with it than to break off and have to come back and start trailing through 'Euston Station' again another night.

People tend to identify a ghost with one particular place in the house and to think of him or her as remaining there at all times. This is not true. I first discovered this on a summer's afternoon. I had been following Elwyn from one room to another in a house alleged to be haunted, when suddenly in one of the bedrooms he stiffened, as he very often does, and pronounced: 'Yes there is a spirit presence here.' Then he moved towards the corner between the door and the wardrobe and added, 'She is a woman spirit and this is her favourite place, this corner between the door and the wardrobe.' Then as an anticlimax, he added: 'But she is not here now. I doubt very much if she is even in the house at this present moment.' They do move around. Apparently they don't go to the trouble of leaving the Spirit world for the Earth world just in order to sit in the corner between a door and a wardrobe in a bedroom.

Elwyn and I had a wonderful example of this kind of thing some years later. A Mrs Harris from the Dwyfor area rang to ask for help, and told me her story. Her husband had been invalided out of the coal-mining industry. Now, with his lungs full of coal dust, he was confined to a downstairs bed surrounded by oxygen cylinders and a maze of rubber pipes.

Mrs Harris had two daughters, Megan and Laura. Megan, very much against her parents' wishes, had married a man they described as a roughneck and a scrounger. Nevertheless they had used their savings to buy her and her husband a house. Two children were born to them, but relations between the husband and the in-laws did not improve. After a quarrel, during which he called Mrs Harris an interfering old cow, he forbade her access to the house and warned Megan that she was never again to take the children to see their grandparents.

For years there was little contact between the two families except when Megan and the children 'accidentally' met Mrs Harris on the High Street. Then the Harrises heard that Megan was ill. Neighbours came to say that she had cancer, and that she looked awful. Mrs Harris called at her daughter's house and the husband opened the door. He told her that she was not wanted, that he was perfectly capable of looking after his own wife without her help.

Megan died, and after her funeral he left the village, taking the children with him, but leaving the house with dishes piled high in the kitchen sink and soiled beds unmade. No one could understand why they had left in such a hurry, never to be seen again. Months later Mrs Harris and some neighbours cleared the house of its furniture and Mrs Harris commissioned the local estate agent to sell it.

In the meantime Laura, the elder daughter, who lived in Liverpool, was in the process on divorcing her husband. She wrote to ask if Megan's house was still unsold and, if so, whether she could rent it until she found a place of her own. The Harrises agreed. But almost the first night Laura slept in the house there was trouble. There were moanings and groanings in the night, stairs creaked and, although it was a breathless summer night, doors banged angrily. But it was not so much the creaking and the banging that troubled her. It was the utter depression and sadness that permeated the whole place and the deep, soulful sighs that made sleep impossible. After two nights she packed her bags and joined her parents in their cottage in the village. The 'For Sale' notice went up again, and this time a young couple showed an interest in buying the property.

It was at this stage that Mrs Harris rang me to tell me she was worried. Now that there was a possibility of the house being bought by strangers, she had started to wonder if the sad ghost that had haunted Laura could be her sister Megan, trying to tell her how very unhappy she had been in that house over the years, living with her awful husband. Even worse, could it be that Megan was now earthbound and confined to this house of torture until someone came to release her? Mrs Harris was not prepared to sell the house until she was assured that Megan was safe.

I called to plan a team visit. When Mrs Harris went to the kitchen to make a pot of tea, her husband beckoned me to his bedside. 'It's not Megan,' he gasped. 'I keep telling her Megan comes to see me every week when the rest have gone to bed. Sometimes she comes twice. Megan is quite happy now. My chest is always better when Megan is here.'

When Elwyn joined us the following week we met at Megan's old house. Mrs Harris and Laura had walked up from their cottage and were there waiting for us. Elwyn 'felt' whatever it was immediately. He told me afterwards that it was something very powerful. He then walked to the window of the little front parlour. 'Looking out of this window I can feel peace and tranquillity,' he said. 'I can see a tiny little garden or rather a tiny little grass lawn peppered with daisies and buttercups and in the middle there is a little diamond-shaped plot and it is full of daffodils.' I looked through the same window but all I could see was a tarred road with cars on each side.

When Elwyn described the little garden Mrs Harris said, 'But that is our garden at the cottage. We have lovely daffodils in the spring, and they are in a kind of diamond-shaped plot.'

'In that case,' said Elwyn, 'I think we would get better results if we were all to move from here to your cottage.' He whispered to me: 'I wonder if Megan will come down with us to the cottage?'

Mrs Harris and Laura both climbed into the back of Elwyn's car – I was going to drive down in my own. Just as we were about to move off Elwyn wound down his car window and said quietly to me: 'It's my car she's picked and she's sitting as large as life beside me on the front seat.'

Mrs Harris's idea of ghosts was similar to most people's – that they stay in the same place, at crossroads, in churchyards or in the libraries of old castles, to frighten people. But the old man was quite right – it was not Megan sighing in the house. Megan came to visit him once a week –

she and her father had always been close. Yesterday's people do that. They visit us, they move around, they meet people, just as we do on a day's outing, and then they travel back again. It is these spirits, and particularly the specially trained teacher spirits, that tell the Spiritualists about dying and death. This of course is why they are able to say, 'We have no beliefs – We know.'

Elwyn told me afterwards that there was something very ugly and very powerful in Megan's old house, and that it wasn't Megan. However, the sale went through and the young couple moved in, and as far as we know they are still there. The probability is they have heard neither groan nor creak in that house.

There is one principle in this 'ghostology' business that is constant. 'Ghosts cannot manifest themselves to Earth-dwellers without the aid of a Spirit-world guide to hasten their departure and an earth medium-guide to allow them to re-enter earth. So Laura must have been the medium who had unwittingly opened the earth door for Megan and the other nasty spirit. Megan's father must also be a sensitive, otherwise Megan could not have visited him every week. I later found that the whole Harris family had this strong trait. To the faint-hearted I can say with certainty, that if you are not a sensitive, and you do not share a house with a sensitive or a mediumistic person, you need never fear that you will see a ghost. That is the good news. The bad news is that computers have worked out that about one in four of the population is sensitive enough to enable a spirit to enter their home.

I don't think I am sensitive but for over 40 years I have, with the help of gifted friends, been seeing and talking to ghosts, and I have been counselling ghosts who died without resolving some of their earth problems. So if Spiritualists can say 'We have no beliefs – we have knowledge,' so can I. It is because of this knowledge that I dare venture to write a book on 'How to Die,' and to pass on to others the little knowledge I have gleaned.

I remember vividly how my association with ghosts began. I had been appointed Director of Social Work for the diocese. My office was in Bangor and I had been told that part of my duties were to help busy parish priests with specialist problems. I had not been in my new office a week when the first special problem arrived. It was a phone message from the wife of a clergyman friend of mine, and she was in great panic. David her husband, was out visiting and she had no idea how to contact him. Half an hour earlier, a young couple had arrived at the vicarage wanting to see him because they had come home from work together and found they could not unlock either the front or the back door of their house. They had looked through the kitchen window to find that someone or something had smashed their furniture and crockery. Both doors were locked, and so were all the windows, and the burglar alarm had not gone off; they knew this was something that required a priest and not a policeman, and they were not going to move from the vicarage drive until the vicar arrived. And, said his poor wife, 'When David does eventually arrive he will be scared stiff – he is terrified of ghosts.' But David and I were lucky. I had heard that a medium from Manchester had recently retired to Anglesey and that he was a bit bored with retirement. He was delighted to take the young couple and their poltergeist off our hands.

After this there followed many vigils in haunted houses throughout the diocese. There were others as well as David who were afraid. There were also those who were convinced that the spirit presence in there home brought with it some kind of sourness and bitterness. One housing association blamed a spirit for making the most obnoxious smells in a block of flats they were about to let!

When I retired some years ago I wrote a book about my experiences. It was called *The Holy Ghostbuster: A Parson's Encounters with the Paranormal*, (published by Element Books, 1996). My intention was to describe my experiences over the years and to give a cross-section of examples of the different kinds of ghosts I had seen, met and talked to. I spoke of earthbound ghosts, and of smelly ghosts, and of ghosts that moved house with the family when the husband got a new job. I was absolutely amazed at the reaction to this book. People from all over the country wrote to thank me for the comfort they had received reading it. Many were practising Christians and regular church-goers. Many of them commended me for being brave enough to say the things I had said in the book. I had the distinct impression that they regarded the Afterlife as a 'no go' area in the church, and that clergymen discouraged people from talking about this kind of thing. It was sufficient for lay people to know their dear ones were 'at rest' and for children to know that Grandpa had 'gone to Jesus'.

I would like to quote from just a few of the letters I received.

Your book should be made compulsory reading for all members of the Church Synod.

JB, Manchester

Thank you for sharing with us your experiences. Quite a brave thing to do whilst still associated with the church.

LT, Harpenden

I feel I have been slowly led along a path which may lead eventually towards spiritual enlightenment.

GB, Strathclyde

I don't think I have ever enjoyed reading a book as much as I have enjoyed yours. It has not only given me great pleasure in reading but great comfort too in believing there is something to look forward to at the end – and nothing to fear.

SW, West Midlands

Please write another, not about ghosts but about a more important subject – about Heaven.

NH, Dublin

As the letters kept arriving I felt very much like the lady in the television advertisement whose nose kept growing bigger as she took the credit for baking a shop-bought cake. I had thought of *The Holy Ghostbuster* as just a book about ghosts and my experiences with spirits from the beyond. I had no idea so many people, many of them practising Christians, had such fears and were so mixed-up in their belief about the Afterlife.

I know this must sound peculiar to many, and I wouldn't blame anyone for asking what kind of a man could a parish priest for over 50 years and yet be unaware of how abysmally ineffective and impotent was the teaching of his Church about life after death. In mitigation I must tell you a little about myself. I was for 40 years the vicar of a lovely, small, one-church country parish. Every Sunday I preached to a small but rather select congregation: on some Sundays I could have present a barrister, four solicitors, two college professors, a police superintendent, a titled lady and a bevy of teachers. They never asked me about doctrine or the Church's teaching. If they wanted to know anything about the Church's dogma they would refer to a Christian bookshop and buy a book about it. Monday to Friday I was in my office in Bangor, dealing mostly with adopters and unmarried mothers, and during the later years with drug addicts and alcoholics. It was what happens now, not what happens after death, that was important to my midweek 'congregation'. The knowledge I needed in my dealing with them was of psychology and sociology.

By the time I had reached the age when one becomes curious about the afterlife, I had mingled so much with Spritualist friends that I could say with them 'I no longer believe – I know.' I was all right Jack, and I stupidly believed that everyone else was too. So I can say, with my hand on my heart, that until I received all those letters and phone calls, and until people stopped me in Bangor High Street, I never knew of this theological void and the spiritual hunger it caused so many people. I then felt I had to fill this void and so I decided to write this book and call it *Yesterday's People*.

2   The Death of a Vicar

People have been talking, writing and theorizing about what happens after we die since the beginning of time. But there is nothing to be gained by just talking about it. Someone has to do something. So tomorrow I would like you to join me in reading my obituary in my favourite newspaper, the *Liverpool Daily Post*:

> Roberts, Aelwyn (Reverend), aged 77. Peacefully at home in Llandegai. Loving husband, father and grandfather. Sometime vicar of the parish. Body to be cremated in preparation for burial at St Tegai's Church at a date to be announced later.

There! In the same way that many medical researchers inject all sorts of chemicals and toxins into their bodies so that they can observe the results, I, a retired vicar, have made myself dead. I have done this so that I, and others who care to join me, can watch and observe what really happens to the dead body under the white sheet.

I expect that an experienced researcher would have a rough idea how he would feel after consuming a cocktail of chemicals and toxins. It must also be true that a parish priest of 50 years has a good idea of what happens to a dead body in a household – at least during the first few days and until its actual disposal.

The doctor is the first to be summoned, and he looks and tests. It is not long before he packs his bag again. He mumbles something about 'It was his heart – he wouldn't have suffered.' You will find that not even the doctor is quite at ease in the presence of death, because even this busy man as he leaves, feels obliged to make some kind of inane remark like 'Nice old chap. I liked him.'

Mind you, it is my physical body lying on the hearthrug that he is looking at. *I* have been standing behind the sofa all the time he has been here but, he didn't notice me. I even went up close to him and shouted in his ear, 'Good morning, Doc!' but he didn't seem to hear me. He just prodded the old body on the floor, and tested it with his stethoscope. Then he put on his special funereal face to tell my wife that there was nothing he could have done, and I thought I saw the quick glance towards the heavens that doctors give when they break the news to the family that someone is dead. The formula is: 'There is nothing more that the medical profession can do', and the quick glance to the heavens suggests, 'It is not us. We, like you, would have liked to have him alive, but it is the powers that be up there that caused this.'

I want to tell him, 'Don't apologize, old chap. I, Aelwyn, who used to occupy that old body, am still here'. But there is no point. He wouldn't hear. Anyway, he has gone now, leaving the two or three family members unfortunate enough to have been caught up in this death syndrome shaking their heads and saying, 'God, what happens now?' I myself found that the passing over was not too difficult; I can still think and reason. It is my little family that is in panic. It think one of them is crying – well not crying perhaps, but looking very sad and very worried. I wish I could tell them not to be sad on my account, and to ring up the vicar because in situations like this it is always good to talk.

And, if this is not possible, there is always the undertaker. He can be found in the Yellow Pages and invariably comes quickly when summoned. Newspapers and journals from time to time describe undertakers as people who claim very high remuneration; they sometimes insinuate that they may even take advantage of people in their sorrow. But people suffering from the trauma of death in the home will find them invaluable. They have an encyclopaedic knowledge of death, and 1001 ideas on how to make funerals more bearable. They know the men who work in the crematorium by name. They know the hymn 'Abide with Me' by its clinical name of 'A and M 27', and that the tune Crimond can be found on page 512 of the Hymnal. They can supply a coffin and, mercy of mercies, know how to wash and dress the corpse and place it in the coffin.

This man, who moments before was a stranger, soon becomes a friend – very nearly a kinsman. He orders the flowers, he arranges the hymn sheet with the vicar. He is so gentle, and so respectful, and he does not speak of death, but of passing away or passing over. He speaks in soft metaphors. For a bereaved person not to pay, or to even begrudge paying, the undertaker's bill after the funeral, could be likened to a kidney transplant patient begrudging his surgeon's fee once he was off dialysis.

And yet unlike the gravedigger, the sexton and the embalmer, the undertaker, this 'general practitioner in the art of burying the dead' is a comparative newcomer to the labour market. I remember an octogenarian friend of mine, who lives in the neighbouring village of Llanllechid, telling me that the biggest funeral he had ever seen in his life was that of Owen Caerau in 1956. Owen was a quarryman and a bachelor, and lived with his mother on their smallholding called 'Caerau'. And there was no doubt about it, he had a thing about death and about the burial of the dead. When he heard of a death in the village, he would put on his second-best suit and visit the family to offer his condolences. Before leaving the house he would offer to 'undertake' the arrangements of the funeral for them. There would be no charge. This kind man would explain that he offered this service instead of a wreath. He would see the parson; he would see the gravedigger; he would fetch the death certificate; he would commission a carpenter to make the coffin and supervise the price. He would also order the flowers for the family and decide on the kind of hearse required and its price, and the number of limousines that were to be hired; or, where there was need, he would solicit friends and neighbours to see if there were any who would allow the use of their cars on the big day. In those days when quarrymen possessed neither car nor telephone, Owen often had to take a day or two of unpaid leave from his quarry – and yet there would still be no charge; it was all 'instead of a wreath'.

The great day was invariably a Saturday. Half an hour before the time of the service Owen would present himself at the house of mourning, in a luxurious suit of braided black velvet with a lace handkerchief in its breast pocket. It would be his task to seek out the more distant members of the family, newly arrived by trains and buses, and to ask them if they wished to view the body before the service began. It would be on his instruction that the coffin lid would finally be screwed in place by the carpenter, and it would be at his nod, and at his nod only, that the minister would invite the congregation to join him in prayer.

The mourners waiting outside the house would look to Owen's black-gloved hand and silver-knobbed cane for their instruction as to whether to march together in double or quadruple order, or whether, as in the funeral of a public figure – a councillor or alderman – to take the eight-abreast formation. This proud princely figure of a master of death would always head the procession. As he came abreast of the local policeman on point duty, the stick in his hand would twitch imperceptibly and the policeman would stand to attention and salute; sometimes the cane's ferrule would twirl the reluctant cap of a gawping schoolboy high into the air.

When Owen Caerau, the amateur undertaker, died in 1956

most of the families in the valley owed him a great debt and turned out to repay it in the way he would have wished. On the day of his funeral, neighbouring parsons and ministers, even the bishop and moderator, turned out to pay their last respects to Owen. And that was why Owen Caerau's funeral was the largest held within living memory in the Ogwen Valley.

But enough of the olden days. Owen Caerau's professional successor is now in attendance at the vicarage in Llandegai. I left instructions about the way I wanted to have my body buried, including the unusual request that it be taken to the crematorium, privately and without a service, to be made ready for burial as soon as convenient after death. I don't think I was ever able to think of a crematorium as a chapel or a place of religion. It was always for me a place where local authority workers were engaged preparing dead bodies for disposal. These men, using expert knowlege, would reduce human bodies to about half a cubic foot in volume, and so make them more manageable and hygienic for the day of burial. I had, I realize now, always felt a bit piqued that the men from the crematorium did not wear overalls in their place of work. They always wore black suits and ties and would stand to attention and bow low over the catafalque. In some places the crematorium staff would wear black gowns or cassocks like those worn by ministers of religion. It was as if these manual workers were somehow trying to usurp the office of a priest. That is why I requested that my body be taken to the crematorium, not for burial but so that it might be made ready for a proper religious burial at my parish church.

It will be interesting, from my newly dead vantage point, to see whether they carry out their work in their black suits or in their overalls, and whether they bow to the catafalque when there are no mourners around to see them.

It will take an hour of fierce flame to dispose of the body and the coffin. The undertaker may offer to help with the scooping of the ashes from the oven when it is sufficiently cool. What will remain are the large knee and femur joints. These must be put through what the men in black suits call the coffee grinder and then poured into standard-sized containers. The remaining ash will be gathered up with brush and ladle so that all the contents of the stainless steel oven end up being put into the casket.

And of course whilst all this is going on, the adults in the family will worry about how to tell the grandchildren that Grandad is dead. But there is no need to worry. Children and old people are least vulnerable to death. Children do not need to know or understand the creed or the teaching of the Church in such matters. They have their own ideas of what has happened. I remember when Patrick, my grandson, was four years of age, his paternal grandfather died. He soon resolved the matter to his own satisfaction. He told me quite seriously that it was God Himself who cooked all the dinners in Heaven, but that it was Jesus who distributed them to those who had crossed over. And now, according to Patrick, his grandfather was the one specially picked to help Jesus distribute the dinners, and at night, after a very busy day, Jesus and his grandfather would sleep together in bunk beds. I don't think my co-grandfather was a member of any church or chapel, but Patrick didn't seem to think this mattered a great deal – after all, he had been a smashing Grandpa.

That was Patrick's theory of life after death. It seems unlikely to me that out of the billions of people who have died over the millenniums, Patrick's grandfather would be the one picked to be Jesus's personal assistant – or indeed that spiritual bodies need carnal sustenance. But I can't prove that Patrick was wrong.

Proof is a very funny thing. All through the centuries, holy men and women have tried to prove the existence of God to others. They know He is there: they have spoken to Him; they have received help and comfort from Him; some of them say they have even seen Him. But they have failed miserably to prove to others that He is there. There is no

Darwin, Einstein or Thomas à Kempis who can walk up to the blackboard in any university lecture theatre and write down the 'proof of God' formula.

For the greater part of my 77 years on this earth I have found it easy to believe that the universe was created by an intelligent being. Some call this intelligent being Allah, others Jehovah, others the Higher Being. I call him my heavenly father. But I have never been able to prove from the pulpit or to a confirmation class that this heavenly father of mine really exists or that it was He who created the universe.

Mind you, there's nothing one-sided about this. When aetheists argue the non-existence of God, they too are unable to prove to others what they so fervently believe themselves. When they are asked to explain who created the world if it was not God, they are reduced to saying that it was one massive gaseous explosion that brought it into being. They are able to show the great scars on the face of the universe caused by this explosion. They can even trace the passage of these gases between the worlds. But they cannot tell us who or what created the gas that caused the explosion in the first place.

So I am not going to be able in this book, or any other book, to prove that there is life after death. I can only do what others are doing – provide sufficient evidence for *believing* that there is life after death.

I live in the Snowdonia National Park. High up in small crevices on the Carneddau and Glyder Mountains, grow tiny little flowers, many of them never to be seen by the human eye. If it is possible to speak to flowers after one is dead, perhaps I shall ask them: 'What is your purpose on this earth, little flowers?' And perhaps they will answer me: 'We are here as part of the evidence for believing in God, sir.'

Someone else who lived and worked in the place where these little mountain flowers grow was our friend Owen Caerau, the amateur undertaker. He never had need of their testimony. He believed implicitly that the souls of the neighbours and friends he was burying would go to Heaven.

The souls of those evil murderers and rapists that he read about in the *Liverpool Weekly Post* would just as certainly go to Hell.

Owen would bow his head, put his hands together and close his eyes tightly like a child when the vicar read the burial service:

> In the faith of Christ, and believing that our brother is in the hands of God, we commit his body to the ground, earth to earth, ashes to ashes, dust to dust, in sure and certain hope of the resurrection to eternal life.

Although the vicar did not specify whether the hope in question was hope that the body would resurrect, or the soul would resurrect – or both the body and the soul. Owen liked to believe he meant both soul and body. It was, he would remind himself, when the vicar was committing the body to ground that he said the words about the resurrection: 'We commit his body to the ground in sure and certain hope of resurrection to eternal life.'

When Owen had first mentioned to the vicar that he wished to become a volunteer undertaker, the vicar had taken him to church for instruction. 'Owen,' he had said, 'the body must always be carried into the church feet first. The coffin will be placed on the trestles already laid in the chancel, with the feet towards the altar, and remain there until the end of the service. After the singing of the second hymn, or at a given sign from the vicar, the undertaker will summon the pallbearers to carry the coffin to the churchyard, seeing to it that it is turned so that the body will again have the feet pointing to the point of destination.'

The vicar had also said that all churches were built facing east and that the altar would always be found beneath the east window. Similarly all Christian graves ran parallel with the church, east to west. The vicar had stressed that the coffin should be placed in the grave with the feet towards the east. He had not said so in so many words, but Owen had deduced that this was so that on the last day, that dreadful Day of Judgement, all the dead of Llanllechid would rise facing east – the direction from which the Lord would come to judge the quick and the dead. And this was not just a local custom; it is something done in all Christian churches to this day.

Owen the slate quarryman, would also have known of the custom that prevailed in Blaenau Ffestiniog, another slate quarry village, 25 miles away. In this parish, if a workman had to have a leg or arm amputated after an accident – and this seemed to happen very often – the limb would be buried in the local churchyard and the place marked with a slate with the person's initials carved on it. When that person himself died, perhaps 20 years later, the body would be buried in the same grave. There would not have been a single person in Blaenau Ffestiniog at this time who required a parson to tell him why. It was so that, at the Day of Judgement, he could stand up whole before his Creator. Only a fool would have invested money to build a crematorium in Blaenau Ffestiniog in those days – there would have been no customers. It was too much to ask anyone to believe that a resurrected body could rise out of a boxful of ashes.

Belief in the resurrection of the body at this time was understandable. There was a hymn to support this view – hymn 575 in the 1916 edition of *Hymns Ancient and Modern*. It was a very respectable hymn written by Mrs Alexander, who had published in the same book her other hymn, 'All things bright and beautiful'. Hymn 575 reads:

> Within the churchyard, side by side,
> Are many long low graves;
> And some have stones set over them,
> On some the green grass waves.
>
> Full many a little Christian child,
> Woman, and man, lies there;
> And we pass near them every time
> When we go in to prayer.

They cannot hear our footsteps come,
They do not see us pass;
They cannot feel the warm bright sun
That shines upon the grass.

They do not hear when the great bell
Is ringing overhead;
They cannot rise and come to Church
With us, for they are dead.

But we believe a day shall come
When all the dead will rise,
When they who sleep down in the grave
Will ope again their eyes.

For Christ our Lord was buried once,
He died and rose again,
He conquer'd death, He left the grave;
And so will Christian men.

So when the friends we love the best
Lie in their churchyard bed,
We must not cry too bitterly
Over the happy dead;

Because, for our dear Saviour's sake,
Our sins are all forgiven;
And Christians only fall asleep
To wake again in Heav'n.

But we mustn't blame Mrs Alexander. This was the understanding of her time. Ministers of religion might not have been preaching the resurrection of the flesh, but their congregations certainly believed it, and it was not just an unofficial understanding. The dogma of resurrection of the body is a part of the credo of the Catholic churches – those which share the same seven sacraments, the same threefold ministry and the same three creeds. Three main Christian churches do this: the Roman Catholic Church, the Orthodox Churches and the Anglican Church. The three creeds that form the basis of belief in these churches are the Apostles'

Creed, the Nicene Creed, and the Athanasian Creed, and they are used in their liturgy. During the service the priest invites members of the congregation to stand and to say together the declaration of their faith. On Trinity Sunday and certain other Sundays, the creed that is recited by the congregation in every Catholic church, from Rome to Canterbury to Istanbul, and throughout the Christian world, is the Athanasian Creed. It begins with the words: 'Whosoever will be saved; before all things it is necessary that he holds the Catholic faith.' There then follows an outline of the tenets that must be held, and then come the words:

> At whose [Jesus's] coming all men shall rise again with their bodies and shall give account of their own works. And they that have done good shall go into life everlasting: and they that have done evil into everlasting fire.

It then ends quite blandly: 'This is the Catholic faith: which except a man believe faithfully he cannot be saved.'

There is nothing tacit about that. It is no use arguing that the creed was written hundreds of years ago and is now old fashioned, nor that I am quoting from the 1662 Prayer Book. I stood up in St Tegai's Church, Llandegai, with others on Trinity Sunday this year, and we were all required to recite the words 'all men shall rise again with their bodes' during the service. It sounds so illogical – the 'earth to earth' part of the burial service, covering the body with half a ton of soil, or reducing it to 2kg of dust, and then asking us to recite together, in church, that we believe 'we shall rise again with our bodies'.

But the Church is like that. The Church is illogical. It has always amazed me that throughout the period we call Lent, and right up to Easter Day, flowers are prohibited in church. I don't think there is any law govering this; it is just that the vicar (or Reverend father) says, 'No flowers in Lent.' And yet this is the period when God is most lavish with his flowers.

Wave upon wave of snowdrops, crocuses, daffodils and hyacinths follow each other in this March–April floral bonanza. But the bishops still seem to say: 'God can do whatever he likes on his own patch, but inside our churches it is still "No flowers in Lent."'

And there is another illogical thing. Every Christian church throughout the world has, on or above its altar, a cross or crucifix. This is presumably so that worshippers can be reminded, and focus their minds on the fact, that we worship the Christ Crucified. Whatever the Church season, be it Lent or Advent, Easter, Christmas or Ascension, the cross remains on the altar with it message: 'We worship Christ crucified.' But when Good Friday – the actual day of the crucifixion – comes, you will find that someone has been round and taken the cross from the altar and put it away in the vestry safe, or that the evening before, the vicar, has put a purple hessian sack over it so that the congregation cannot see it or use it for meditation.

So it could be that with the same kind of illogical thinking, when Church scholars and theologians say 'shall rise again with their bodies', they really mean that we will arise in a new spiritual body and not in the battered old wrinkly one in the coffin.

But if that is what they mean, then all I can say is that nobody at any time bothered to tell me.

3   I, Aelwyn

———

Meanwhile, back in the vicarage at Llandegai. It is now three days since I died. Nothing much has happened during those first three days. My physical body is still there, although by now thankfully transferred into a coffin, but what do we mean by a physical body? The chemist would tell us with fair accuracy that the main components of a man weighing 70kg (154lb or 11 stone) are:

	Percentage	Kilograms
Water	70	49
Fat	15	10.5
Protein	12	8.4
Carbohydrate	0.5	0.35
Other minerals	2.5	1.75

But what else do we know about this body of mine? In the old days grandmothers used to reply in a riddle when children asked them their age. They used to say: 'I am as old as my tongue, and a little older than my teeth.' But we now know this is not true because biologists tell us that our bodies wear out completely every seven years and a new ones grow to replace it. So that body in the coffin over there is not really 77 years of age, it is only seven. My latest body, the one that died the other day, is probably Aelwyn Mark 11 or Aelwyn

Mark 12. I have during my life used up to 11 different hearts, 22 kidneys, and 11 or 12 different brains. I have reincarnated every seven years. Biologists can prove that this cell change occurs. I am no scientist, and I have no idea how they do this. But we don't need biologists to prove that we cast away our dead skin cells. We are throwing these away all over the house. We scatter them so extravagantly that some people are even made to sneeze and develop different allergic reactions because of them.

So what is the implication of all this? I graduated from St David's College, Lampeter, in 1940. I sat several three-hour examinations, for which I used my memory to recall a great deal of information that I had collated over many years. I used my brain to reason and argue in different dissertations until it was tired for several days afterwards. But scientists tell me the brain I used for the examination when I was 21 is not the same as the one that is now inside the cranium of the body in the coffin. I have only owned and used the coffin brain for the last seven years.

Again, I remember that as teenagers in Blaenau Ffestiniog my friends and I would go swimming in the river's black pool every day in the summer. Diving from the different high ledges gave us a particular thrill. Those who were unable to swim would still dive in and hope that the thrust of their dive would enable them to reach the other side. Eddy couldn't swim, and on one occasion he miscalculated his distance and popped up in the deep end. I dived in and dragged him the few yards to safety.

I saved Eddy's life that day But the teenage legs that kicked my body off the cliff edge into the water have long gone. The arms with which I dragged my panicking friend from the water have been dead for many a long year. This last body of mine had nothing whatsoever to do with Eddy's rescue. Yet one thing is quite certain: it was I, Aelwyn, who rescued Eddy. It was I, Aelwyn, who dived into that cold pool over 60 years ago. I can still remember the shivering we both did afterwards.

So what are we observing? In the coffin there is Aelwyn's chemical body. During the last 77 years these cells, millions of them, have been changing and making themselves new again. Only recently it had been quite obvious that the renewed ones have not been of as good a quality as the old ones. Which is another way of saying that latterly I had been feeling my age.

It was I, Aelwyn, who passed my exams many years ago. It was I, Aelwyn, who saved my friend from drowning many years ago. But the body that is now lying in the coffin had no part in these activities. This is a difficult concept. The ego or 'I' seems to have been doing all sorts of worthwhile things over the last 70 years, but only by using several different but related bodies.

I still remember my primary school maths, and how we were all stumped when we had to deduct from a number an amount greater than itself. 'Seven from six won't go,' we used to wail in chorus. The teacher would then encourage us to borrow ten and we could then chant together again, 'Seven from sixteen equals nine', and the problem would be solved. The teacher would then warn us that if we continued with our calculation the borrowed ten would have to be repaid. I mention this because I think we too have come to a 'won't go' situation in our thinking and must 'borrow ten' before we can advance further. 'Borrowing ten' allows us to assume that there has been an 'I', an ego, a personality or a soul lodged in our various changing bodies since the day we were born. It has survived all the chemical changes of the body. We have never seen it. The surgeon's knife has failed to reveal it. But goodness me, we have talked about it and boasted about it all our lives – it is always 'I did this' and 'I did that.'

I have looked out through the now-closed eyes of the tired old body in the coffin for over 77 years – different eyes, but the same 'I' looking through them. I have listened to what other people said to me through the body's ears – different ears but the same 'I' listening. And throughout my life it is that 'I' that has reprogrammed and tuned the wonderful brain-computer the old body had. But I didn't merely look through those eyes, or listen through those ears, or think thoughts through those brain cells. It was I who trained those eyes to see the things I wanted them to see. I manipulated those ears to hear what I wanted them to hear and I cultivated and programmed that wonderful multi-recycled brain to think what I wanted it to think.

So we really need two observation posts – one from which to observe the 70kg seven-year-old chemical mass that is in the coffin and the other to see what is to happen to the 77-year old 'I' who has been recently evicted from his physical home.

There seems to be some extra activity in the house today. Something at long last is about to happen. Had I died a Jew or a Muslim, the funeral would have been performed the same day. Buddhists, however, believe in a reincarnated life after death and that the old body should not be too speedily discarded. After death it is washed and perfumed and made clean for the resurrection. There is also a period of rest following the death and there is a day of reckoning. After the reckoning the ego has another go at another earth life. So the Buddhist belief is in some ways similar to that of the Christian. Their ideas about death are similar, including the period of rest to await the judgement. Even the idea of reincarnation is not as incongruous as it seems, because the Christian Church also believed in reincarnation up until the Council of Constantinople in AD 553. It took over 500 years for Christians to discard this idea that we live more than one life on this planet.

When they finally get me down to the crematorium, my own parish priest, using his Book of Common Prayer, will say:

> And we are mortal, formed of the earth
> And unto earth shall we return.

If I was being buried by a Muslim mullah, he would read over my coffin the words:

> From the earth did we create you
> And into it shall you return.

The similarity makes one feel quite ecumenical.

The rabbi would have tried to have my old body in the grave before sunset the same day. This is not because the Jews believe for one minute that the material body has ceased to be of any further use. They do not favour cremation, because they believe that after death the body goes to a sort of limbo, a place of waiting, or an undefined sort of place in between Heaven and earth. There is a feeling that it might be prudent to treat the physical body with respect, because it is just possible it might be needed again in Heaven. There doesn't seem to be a hard and fast rule about these things. I am sure that if I were a Jew or a Muslim I would be just as unhappy with their teaching of what happens to me after death as I am of the explanation proffered by the Christian Church.

Hindus, like Buddhists, believe quite simply that when you die in this world you will come back to it again and again to live further lives. The left wing of the 'reincarnation party' even goes as far as to say that one might come back as a worm or a rat. But the more liberal like to believe that one will still come back in human form in the next life, though not necessarily of the same sex.

As one would suspect, disposing of the physical body is of little importance to people of this belief. If you are dead and going to live another life, you will be given another body. And let's face it, if you lived an antisocial life in your last existence you may not have a great deal of use for a human body in the next world. A good firm spider body or a snail body with an extra firm shell would perhaps be more practical.

For Buddhists, funerals are more secular than religious.

Buddha gave instructions to his priests and monks not to become too involved in the practical side of burial. They were to leave the manual acts of burial to lay people. This is more or less what happens today. The monks come along and say a few prayers and receive their food offerings. They also do one other thing which is interesting: they place a white cloth over the body. Because they believe the body is polluted, only they, who are immune to pollution, can remove the cloth, which is meant to absorb the impurities, or sins, from the body.

But not even the monks are allowed to touch the dead body during its lying in state, and the reason for this ban is quite clear. The body is not to be disturbed during the period when the *bar-do* body (the 'I, Aelwyn' part) leaves the material body.

So in Buddhism after death the body – the impermanent physical body – is stripped and washed clean by neighbours and family, and then bent into the embryonic posture. Scarves are tied around it so that it can retain this womb position. And then (and I could not help thinking of poor old Owen Caerau, the amateur undertaker of Llanllechid, when I read this bit), the body is taken out and carried on the undertaker's back as quickly as possible to its place of burning. Owen would have been horrified.

But it is perhaps only the recent translation of *The Tibetan Book of the Dead* that has enabled us to have a true picture – or really pictures – of the various funeral customs in Buddhist Tibet. There are several different forms of burial. Water burial is for beggars and destitute, possibly because it is so easily carried out. Weights are tied to the body which is then thrown into the sea or river. There is also earth burial, mostly for lepers and those who suffer from plague and other infectious illnesses. If I were a Buddhist monk and not an Anglican priest, my body would be cremated, as cremation is reserved for priests, monks and aristocrats. But the stupa burial is the most grandiose of all. It is reserved for the highest lamas, such as the Dalai Lama and the Tashi Lamas. Their bodies are mummified and their faces painted. Many of the past Dali Lamas have been placed to rest in the Po Ta Palace in Lhasa.

These are burials for specific classes. But perhaps the most gruesome – at least to our Western sensibilities – is reserved for the ordinary citizen. If the Joe Bloggs of Tibet is not a beggar, a leper, a monk or a lama, the only option for him is a sky burial. His body is carried by members of the family to the top of the highest mountain. A fire is lit and handfuls of roasted barley are scattered on it. The smoke and the barley aroma attracts the sacred vultures. Members of the family then proceed with knives to strip the flesh from the bones of the dead person. The bones are crushed and mixed with roasted barley and offered to the vultures. After the bones have been consumed the flesh is offered. Tibetan mourners over hundreds of years had come to understand that if the whole body is offered to the vultures the birds will consume the flesh but leave the bones. It is a cause of great grief to the family if the smallest portion of a loved one's body is left uneaten. So it has been decreed that the bones must be fed to the hungry birds first, followed by the flesh.

I find this anxiety that every tiniest portion by consumed very interesting. There was a time when we had a custom in Wales that served a similar purpose. An elderly lady I met in Waenfawr showed me the very spot where, in her grand-father's day, the villagers would place their offerings for the local 'sin eater'. Up until the mid-eighteenth century many Welsh villagers had their sin eaters. They were men who lived rough, unshaven and unwashed, and dressed in rags. They would live in hovels among the trees and as far away as possible from other people. But they had a very special job to do for the community.

Centuries earlier Martin Luther had warned people not to pray for the dead and not to have masses for them as was the custom in the Church of Rome. The Welsh were among the last in Britain to break away from the Roman Catholic Church, and after the break they didn't quite know how to help their dearly departed without the benefit of candle, prayer or requiem. Presumably the idea of a sin eater stemmed from this problem.

When a man lay dying, his eldest son would be dispatched to ask the village cake lady to bake a 'take-away cake' as fast as she could. This cake was for the sin eater and had to be of the best quality. It was made with white flour and was heavy with fruit and sugar. The dying man's son would carry it with haste from the oven to his father's death chamber, and place it reverently, still warm, on the bare chest of the dying man. The belief was that his sins would escape from his body through his breast and into the newly baked cake. Did this cake serve the same purpose on a hillside farm in Wales as the white linen cloth laid by the Buddhist monks on the chest of a dying man in the mountains of Tibet?

When the man died, the parish clerk would let the village know by ringing the church bell: three rings and a pause for a man, two rings and a pause for a woman, and one ring and a pause for a child. The tolling of the bell would also alert the sin eater. The eldest son would carry the cake to the sin eater's haunt in the village, place it on the appropriate stone and leave. The next day the members of the family would visit the place. There would be great joy if they found that every morsel of the cake had been eaten. This would mean that all their father's sins would have been taken away. The sin eater, who carried the sins of the village, would also now carry the sins of their father. Welsh nonconformist sins were ejected from the dying man's body into the cake, and had in turn been consumed by the poor sin eater. Buddhist sins were ejected into the white cloth, or mixed with the roasted barley consumed by the sacred vultures. And the bereaved families in both Wales and Tibet rejoiced to see that the consummation had been completed.

There is a theory that Welsh people came originally from India and Tibet, but my old body over here is neither Indian or Tibetan. It is the body of a Welsh country parson and that does not prevent it from putrefying after so many days unless it is attended to. Most putrefied bodies usually find their way into the humus, as it says in the funeral service:

> And we are mortal formed of the earth
> And unto earth shall we return.

If evidence of this were needed, the pupils of the 3B biology class could provide it. They would know where to find dead frogs and mice – 3B always do. If such a dead creature were laid out on a secluded patch of the school playground, observers would note that, over a period, it would be drawn, feathers or fur included, into the earth, and the teacher would explain that nature has its own 'undertaker' insects, and its own system of recycling animal bodies into the humus of the earth. It can be argued that, in the same way, a human body is recycled into humus.

But proof is difficult. I have a feeling that a good judge would regard this opinion as rather unsafe if it were based merely on the 3B experiment, even if we added to this the further information that my body is already putrefying after only three days. I have a feeling a good judge would need still more evidence before pronouncing that the physical body is erased and finally eradicated at death, and that it is a vehicle for earth life only.

We must remember that there are many learned people today who *do* believe in the resurrection of the body. All my gypsy friends, who live close to nature and know many of her secrets, believe in it. No gypsy will ever burn the body of a dear one. They will burn his caravan and all his earthly possessions, but not his body. The body is lovingly lowered into a flower-lined grave, and I have a feeling – just a suspicion or a hunch, and I would not like to be quoted on this – that many of the coffins I have seen lowered into gypsy graves have had a few £20 notes and some of the dead person's personal possessions pushed in on the sly at the foot end before they were finally screwed down.

So who are we to believe – the gypsies, who say we should not burn the physical body but bury it very carefully, because after the Day of Judgement we may need it again; or the 3B pupils, who say once we are dead our bodies go back to the earth again just like those of mice and frogs? I don't know. If we put the dead body in a glass coffin and covered it with soil we would be able to see it decaying, so that in years it would have become humus just like those of other creatures. On the other hand, I have seen with my own eyes many ghosts and spoken to many departed spirits over the years, and they look exactly as I remember them in their earth lives. We hear a lot of people say, 'My father came and stood by the kitchen door', or 'I felt there was someone in the room with me; I turned round and there was my mother smiling at me'. Whether they be the spirits of a father, a mother or a neighbour, we recognize them by their outward appearance. Whatever kind of body it is, it looks a lot like the one they used to have.

So I have to say to 3B with their frogs and birds: 'You may be quite right about my old physical body turning to humus, but the evidence also points to the fact that the 'I' part will acquire a new after-death body that will not decompose at all.'

4 *Habeas Corpus*

—

When a child is afraid of the dark, his father will often go into the room with them. Together they will both poke in corners, look under the bed and then comfort each other with the words: 'There is nothing here – nothing to be afraid of.' But in the houses our ghost team visits, we invariably find that there *is* something there. We have to find whatever it is, and also decide whether it is something we ought to fear or not. It is a job that needs to be approached prayerfully.

I remember visiting an isolated farmhouse, the home of a newly married couple. Some weeks before Christmas their sleep was disturbed by a nightly scratching by what they took to be a large mouse or a rat. One week before Christmas the ghost of a horrible monster figure took the bedclothes off the young husband's part of the bed. He had opened his eyes to see this horrible thing leering at him. That freezing cold night this young couple fled half a mile, in their nightclothes, to the house of their nearest neighbour, to plead for shelter. They had sworn that they would never again return to that horrible house.

But they did return, just one week after Christmas, with Elwyn and me. We sat together in the old farmhouse and Elwyn said: 'I can see her. She is a small woman and she has the lovely russet skin of a person used to the outdoors. She is wearing clogs and she has a finely laundered hessian apron covering her black dress.' The young couple gave an exclamation and pointed to Elwyn's left side. And I saw her too – she was standing there, clearly visible, and she was smiling at us. She was no monster; she was a very attractive old lady. She talked to us for a very long time. She told us that she had been the last working tenant of this farm. She told us of her widowhood and of her eventual second marriage. She told us of her regular attendance at the nonconformist chapel and of the feuding between church against chapel during the period leading up to the disestablishment of the Church in Wales. She hated the Episcopal Church and its wretched parish priest. When we asked her where her body had been buried, she just pointed through the window and said, 'Local cemetery.' She also told us that her name was Hannah Roberts.

The following day I visited a couple in their eighties who had lived the whole of their lives in the village where we had met Hannah. I asked them if they could tell me who had farmed Hendre Bach during the First World War. Without hesitation they said, 'William and Hannah Roberts.' I asked them if Hannah was a rather small, pretty, extrovert woman with light hair and smiling eyes, wearing clogs and a hessian apron. They were amazed at my accurate description of her. They were also able to confirm what Hannah herself had already told us, that she had been buried at the local cemetery. They even told us how to find the grave. That afternoon I stood by the grave of Hannah Roberts. The inscription on her tombstone told me she had been buried there for over 40 years, and I was convinced that the Hannah Roberts buried here was the same person I had been talking to in her old home the previous night.

But the important thing about this story is that Elwyn had enabled the young couple to see Hannah for themselves. And after seeing her, they began to wonder why on earth they had thought of her as a leering monster. Now they asked Elwyn to tell her to stay for as long as she wanted, and to feel free to visit at any time.

I remember on another occasion being in a haunted house with my friend Winnie Marshall. Winnie is a real dyed-in-the-wool Spiritualist, a minister of her church, a wonderful healer and clairvoyant, and great to be with when ghosts become too boisterous. On this occasion Winnie said to us: 'I can see a woman in middle age with greying hair and she is dreadfully lame, poor thing. Oh no,' she corrected herself, 'I can see more clearly now. It isn't a limp; the poor woman has got the biggest, crippling club foot I have seen in my life.'

The lady of the house said very quietly: 'That will be Aunt Sarah. She was my husband's aunt. His mother died when he was young and Aunt Sarah took him to live with her. She was the only mother my husband ever knew. She lived with us during the latter part of her life and she died in this house about five years ago.'

'Well, I think she still pops in to see you from time to time,' said Winnie.

I have no doubt that knowing people who delve in and out of the paranormal, who are able to speak to the dead and know about dying and the life beyond has helped me immensely. It has taken away the fear of death. As a matter of fact, there are times when I can feel quite excited about the thought of dying. But I have to add that I still say, like St Augustine: 'But not just yet, Lord.'

However, knowing these people has also posed new problems. I keep asking myself why poor Aunt Sarah was still lumbered with the club foot five years after passing on to the afterlife? And it worries me that a nice old lady like Hannah Roberts could still retain such bitter and hurtful thoughts about a parish priest 40 years after her death.

And there is another thing. Elwyn and I have often seen the same ghost or spirit form using bodies from different times and dressed in clothes from different periods. I remember how we came across one young woman spirit in a garden saying farewell to her betrothed, a young army officer who had been posted to India. Weeks later, when we visited the house again, we met the same spirit, but on this occasion she was an old lady. There was no wedding ring on her finger – she made a point of showing us the ringless finger. When we asked the Curator of Army Records to check the fate of her betrothed, he was able to tell us that, whilst in India, he had been court-martialled and discharged with ignominy from His Majesty's Forces. The young lady's father was a retired colonel, and the court-martialled officer had never dared return to claim his bride.

So I am forced to the conclusion that the souls, egos, spirits or 'I's of those who have died and appear again, always do so in bodies. Yesterday's people are no keener on nudism than most people today. The bodies are worn so that the 'I' can be recognized. The spirit body is outwardly very like the earth body, but without its bulkiness and solidity; they are impervious to doors, walls and solid boundaries.

St Paul tells us, in his wonderful treatise on the Resurrection (I Cor 15), that there is an earthly body *and* a spiritual body, and he goes on to explain the differences between the two (I Cor 15:40–49). But how different are they? As different as the bread and wine of the Eucharist is to the bread and wine on our dining tables perhaps? Churches all over the world believe that Jesus is present in the bread and the wine of Holy Communion. The Anglican Church says that He is present in the bread and the wine in a very real sense; this teaching is called the Doctrine of the Real Presence. The Eastern Orthodox Church calls Communion 'the Mystery', and they too believe that Jesus is present in a very real way in this mystery. The Roman Catholic Church goes a step further. They explain the presence of the Son of God in the bread and in the wine after consecration using the argument of Aristotle, who said that all matter has two main attributes, 'accidents' and 'substance'. The accidents of the bread received in

Communion are those things witnessed by the senses – its whiteness, its roundness, its taste; the accidents of the communion wine are its liquidity, its colour, its taste and its smell. But the substance of matter is a commodity that cannot be discerned by the senses. So, says the Roman Catholic Church, the accidents of the bread and wine in Holy Communion remain the accidents of bread and wine even after consecration. But the substance of the bread is changed at consecration into the substance of the body of Christ, and the substance of the wine is changed to the substance of the blood of Christ. This is called the Doctrine of Transubstantiation.

Could it be that a similar change happens to the body after death? Does it also retain all its recognizable accidents whilst changing its substance? St Paul, the great philosopher, cannot conceive of a soul without a body. In his first letter to the Corinthians, chapter 15, he writes:

> There are heavenly bodies and earthly bodies . . . When the body is buried it is mortal, when raised it is immortal . . . When buried it will be ugly and weak; when raised it will be beautiful and strong. When buried it is a physical body. When raised it will be a spiritual body.

Some religious leaders through the centuries have maintained that the new body is not just something handed out to us at death, in return for the old, discarded body. They believe that we live our earthly lives clothed in two bodies – the Earthly and the Spiritual bodies described by St Paul. At death we merely discard the outward earthly body, and continue our journey in our lighter, more manageable and more beautiful spiritual body. Whenever I think of the idea of wearing two bodies for the whole of our earthly life, I am reminded of the tramps, or gentlemen of the road, of my childhood days. They invariably wore two overcoats, even on the hottest summer days. They knew that the second coat they endured throughout the heat of summer would become a necessity when winter came.

Some of my Spiritualist friends believe that from our birth we are encased in seven separate bodies, one for life on earth, and the other six for our later six lives on ascending planes of existence.

But whether it is two bodies or seven, the consensus of world religious opinion seems to be that the 'I' released from my funny-looking old body in the corner will now be able to reappear in a new spiritual body. I take comfort from the words of St Paul, because he says that mercifully the new one will be more beautiful that one over there in the coffin that I have left to be disposed of by my family.

My own experience of the paranormal has led me to believe that those of us who have crossed over can disguise our beautiful spiritual bodies in order to make ourselves known when we revisit. We can attach a club foot or scar if this becomes necessary. We can appear as a young or an old person, and we can even dress up our bodies in period clothes. And then when we feel like it, we can disappear, clothes and all, through the wall of our old home without creating the slightest damage to the wall or to ourselves.

I am convinced that the ghosts and spirits who make use of earth-bodied mediums and sensitives are able to communicate with those of us still living on earth. I know this because I have talked with them, and I have seen them in the bodies that they have disguised to look like their former earth bodies.

There is nothing new or alarming in this. As a matter of fact, we have only arrived at very much the same conclusion as did the Anglican Church more than 70 years ago.

In 1920, the Lambeth Conference of all the bishops of the Anglican Church throughout the world set up a commission of two archbishops, 30 bishops and many of its top lay scientists to report on the Christian faith and its relation to Spiritualism. The report, when it came, was as dry as dust, but it did say:

It is possible we are on the threshold of a new science which will confirm us in the assurance of a world behind the world we see . . . and that a limit could never be set to the means which God could use to bring man to the realization of a spiritual life.

5 The Afterlife in the Bible

—

What has the Bible to say about what happens to us after death? Surprisingly enough, it says very, very little. There are only a few verses that even mention the Afterlife, and I have a feeling that even these have been taken out of context.

The account a parson is most likely to come up with is the story of Dives and Lazarus. Jesus tells it as a parable. There is a rich man called Dives, who lives sumptuously in his palace and a poor man, Lazarus, who lives in the street under the rich man's window. Dives eats all manner of meats and nourishing foods, and as happened in those pre-finger-bowl days, wipes his fingers between courses on pieces of bread. He then throws the bread through the window to be deftly caught by Lazarus the beggar down below. Both men died. Dives opens his eyes in a place of torment. Looking up, he sees Lazarus being held to Abraham's bosom. He makes a request: 'Please Father Abraham, can Lazarus be sent to fetch a drink for me? I seem to be on fire in this place.' But he is firmly reminded by Abraham that there is a great gulf between the place where he is and where Abraham and his prodigy Lazarus are standing. Abraham also says that this gulf is quite impassable. The rich man then asks for another favour. Please can Lazarus be sent back to earth to warn his five brothers of what could befall them if they do not make better use of their earth lives. Abraham answers: 'Your brothers have the prophets to warn them. That should be enough; there should be no need to send people over from Hades to earth.'

The Church quotes this parable in most discussions about life after death, first perhaps because there is precious little else to quote, and secondly because it does reinforce the 'pie in the sky; Lazarus today, Dives tomorrow' view that the Church has been teaching since the last century. The emphasis is always on the impassable gulf that exists in the life hereafter between those who have done good and those who have done evil. The impassability of this gulf leads quite naturally to the idea of eternal damnation.

When I, wearing my clerical collar, declare that I do not believe in Heaven and Hell as designated places of reward and punishment, the faithful are often horrified. What about Dives, the horrible man who lived such a selfish life? He found himself in a place where even a drop of water on his tongue would have been welcome. And poor Lazarus on the other hand, who had to fight with the dogs for the crumbs this selfish man threw out of the window, finds himself in Heaven.

I never could see the parable in this light. Dives was a rich man enjoying his riches to the full. There is nothing wrong with that; Jesus never condemned any man for being rich. He often stayed at the homes of rich people and dined with them. Lazarus seems to me rather a nondescript character. There is nothing at all in the narrative to say that he was blind or crippled or unable to do a full day's work. He seemed perfectly satisfied to live his life as a dependant of the rich man and would probably guard his pitch very jealously against other beggars. Dives is not described as a bad man and a candidate for Hell fire, nor is Lazarus depicted in the story as a particularly good and saintly man, certainly not as a person worthy of the high honour of being held to eternity in Abraham's bosom. I don't think Jesus was thinking of the

Afterlife when he spoke this parable. His message surely was, 'Don't wait too long before preparing yourselves for death. Get down to it while you are still here on Earth. Seek your salvation now – don't wait until you are dead.' This is an oft-repeated message in the New Testament.

If this parable is to be taken as a demonstration of what is to come, how awfully awful the idea – that if we remain satisfied with a poor, shoddy, crumb-eating Earth life we can be rewarded in the next. And the reward, the top prize, is the honour of being held securely in Abraham's bosom until eternity. God help us! Even the girls when I was child used to scoff at this idea. They used to skip to the rhyme:

> Mary Anne has gone to rest
> Safely now on Abram's breast.
> Which is very nice for Mary Ann
> But not so good for Abraham.

I have always been at a loss to understand the bit about the impassability of the gulf between the living and the dead. Moses and Elijah both tackled this gap fairly effortlessly so that they could be with Jesus on the mountain at His Transfiguration. Even Archbishop Lang's Commission of 1938 was prepared to say in its final report: 'We find that communication of spirits with people on earth is a fact.' My own experiences have led me to believe that we are separated not by an impassable gulf, but by a very, very thin veil or a well-oiled gate.

A short time ago our ghost team answered a call from a farmer and his wife, Steven and Hilda, a couple who were rather frightened because they were being troubled by an army of ghosts. We went to their home and explained the process to them. Elwyn set up his little lamp and sat on his upright chair behind his table and the rest of us started the introductory conversation. But we just could not get Steve and Hilda to join in. They were scared, and obviously embarrassed in their own home. I have never experienced an evening quite like this one. All sorts of characters from the unseen started to come into the light of Elwyn's infra-red lamp. The first one to come was a Richard Owen. From the change in Elwyn's features it seemed that he was probably a good age – 86 he told us afterwards – and he sported a wonderful moustache that really suited Elwyn. Richard sat down with a smile on his face, obviously enjoying being one of a company. When I asked Steven, just to keep the conversation going, how many sheep he kept, he said 52, but old Richard, who had obviously farmed it in previous years, interrupted without being asked and said 94. Steven, however, was not interested. He and Hilda just sat at the end of the settee holding hands, feeling very awkward and wishing the whole thing could be over as quickly as possible. The next spirit to visit us was Richard Owen's vicar. He explained that he was in the habit of popping in to see how Richard was getting on. He didn't seem to be at all put out when he found that on this particular evening his parishioner was entertaining a host of new friends who had been born a few generations after him.

Strangely it was with the today's people that the vicar seemed to want to talk that evening and not with his co-spirit Richard. He talked of his son up at Oxford; he told us he was doing well there and he was very proud of him. Then suddenly he and Richard went off together. It is strange, but ghosts do that kind of thing. When they have had enough, or when they feel like it, they just get up and leave. I have never found out why. It could be that their time is rationed and that the door-keeper allows them to cross on condition that they do not dominate earth meetings.

A new character came. He was different – a newer, fresher ghost, although I don't know how I knew. He came in and walked quite confidently into the infra-red area. It was his hands I noticed first. They were enormous, and as he came in he turned them palm upwards towards us as a sort of salute.

He sat down and he placed one on each knee. And then an amazing thing happened. Shy Steven let go of his wife's hand, jumped on to his feet and actually shouted with joy when he recognized this character: 'Bill Ramston of all people! What the hell are you doing here, you old bugger? What's it like the other side, Bill, with no whisky? It's good to see you – any time, Bill!'

I noticed that throughout Steven's exuberant welcome Bill Ramson was smiling through Elwyn's face.To the question, 'What is it like in Paradise without whisky?' he nodded his head, raised his palms and said, 'It's all right. It's all right.' I think we all would have been a bit more reassured if he had been just a little more enthusiastic about life without his whisky across the Jordan. But we did learn that Bill had only been dead a little over a month, so it could be that 'cold turkey' can be just as exacting in Paradise as it is here on earth.

Steven then turned to his wife and said: 'Look Hilda, it's your father. Can you see him?'

'Yes,' said Hilda very quietly. 'I can see him.'

'Say hello to him then,' said Steven, who was by now quite carried away by events.

'Hello, dad,' said Hilda.

We then saw one of the huge hands being stretched out towards Hilda, and Elwyn said to her: 'I think your father wants to hold your hand.' She dutifully grasped the hand her father was borrowing from Elwyn and they held hands and wept quietly together for a little while.

When Bridget, my daughter, asked Hilda at the end of the evening whether she felt she had been holding Elwyn's hand or her father's, Hilda was very sure of her answer. 'It was my father's hand I was holding,' she said.

Steven told us that Bill Ramson, his father-in-law, had only been dead a month or so. 'It was those hands of his I recognized,' he said. 'Old Bill had enormous hands and he always gesticulated with them. When I saw those upturned palms I just knew it had to be my father-in-law.' In his life he had been a hard man. Even his daughter admitted he was a bully. He had lived a hard-drinking, prodigal life, most of the time apart from his family. Now just four weeks after the passing over, as the undertaker would have said, he was able to say to us with a smile on his face that life on the other side, even without whisky, was 'all right'.

For the small party of people that night, I am sure the sight of old Bill Ramson, with his huge gesticulating hands and his obvious enjoyment at being asked by his son-in-law what it was like the other side without whisky, was a far happier picture of someone who had died than the one of the beggar Lazarus clasped tight to Abraham's bosom.

There is another reference to the Afterlife in the Bible. It is the lovely story of something that happened at the Crucifixion on that hot afternoon on Calvary. One of the thieves who was being crucified with Jesus broke the awful silence to beg a very great favour of him: 'Jesus, let me be with you in thy kingdom (Luke 23:42).' Tradition gives this man the name Dismas. Theologians call him the penitent thief. He is the only man in the scriptures who calls Jesus by his Christian name. Everyone else addresses Him as 'Lord' or 'Master' or 'Rabboni', but this man calls Him just plain 'Jesus'. Some have suggested that the two of them could have been brought up and played together in Galilee, and that as they grew up they both decided to seek a kingdom. Dismas as a Jewish terrorist, dreamt of a kingdom free of Roman domination, while our Lord, even as a boy, was talking of the kingdom of His father. On the cross the failed terrorist turns to his childhood friend and says to Him in effect: 'Jesus my kingdom has turned out to be a washout, please can I have part of the one you used to talk about when we were kids together in Galilee?' And Jesus's answer to him is: 'Today thou shalt be with me in Paradise' (Luke 23:43).

Note that the promise was that they would be together in Paradise, not in Heaven. There is no suggestion of either

Dismas or even our Blessed Lord entering Heaven. Nor is there any suggestion that this thief on the cross should be destined for Hell. Jesus expected that once dead, they would both find themselves together in Paradise. This Paradise seems to be the place of waiting for all who die.

But the story I find most puzzling is that of the resurrection of Lazarus. Lazarus is Jesus's friend. When the news is brought to Him far away that Lazarus is dead, 'Jesus wept'. Then He decides to return, and by forced marches arrives at Lazarus's grave in Bethany, three days after he has been buried. Jesus prepares to bring him back to life again. Mary, Lazarus's sister, pleads with Him not to because she thinks it is too late. 'Leave him,' she says. 'He has been buried three days and by now he stinks' (John 11:39).

But Jesus is determined and He calls out his name. All the people are astounded when they see this linen-clad mummy shuffling his way from the grave into the heat of the sun. Lazarus has been made alive again.

This miracle happened towards the end of Jesus's life on earth. The time of His Crucifixion was drawing near. The raising of Lazarus from the dead could quite easily have hastened the day of His death. This act, witnessed by hundreds of people, must have brought many more to believe in Jesus, and the High Priest and the Pharisees must have felt some urgency to hasten His trial and execution.

We hear nothing more of Lazarus. He was not with Jesus in the Garden of Gethsemane, where He was captured; he was not present at any of his trials. Seeing 'the man risen from the dead' walking about again would surely have stirred up support for Jesus amongst the fickle crowds, and would possibly have confounded the machinations of his enemies. But there was no sign of Lazarus. He was not even standing at the foot of the cross with the others. Mary his sister was there, but not Lazarus. On the morning of the Resurrection, Mary would certainly have told her brother of her experiences at the grave and that Jesus was risen and yet when hundreds of Jesus's followers reported seeing Him during the 40 days before His Ascension, Lazarus is not mentioned as being amongst any one of these groups.

Before he was raised from the dead, Lazarus had been buried for three days. He must in those three days have opened his eyes in Paradise and seen the glory of it, experienced the colours, and the warmth and the love of the place, and the wonderful music. Then his dearest friend came and dragged him back again to the sordid earth life in Bethany. Could it be, I wonder, that Lazarus, like many of us after him, questioned the ways of God, and could not understand what possible reason there could have been for playing what appeared to him to be a cruel trick, particularly as the perpetrator was his friend?

I have often wondered whether Jesus's first act on the morning of the Resurrection was one not reported in the Gospels – a sort of private family act when He went to show Himself first to His mother and to invite her to join Him in Paradise because he felt she had had enough suffering. And was the second call on that day perhaps to his great friend Lazarus – the friend who for some reason unknown to us had had to be dragged from the joy of life in Paradise back to sordid earth again? Was Lazarus too invited to join the little Paradise party on that day? We hear nothing of either the Blessed Mother or Lazarus joining with the other disciples to celebrate the joy of the Resurrection.

One Biblical reference I always seem to be quoting in my defence when discussing the paranormal is the rare occasion when the New Testament describes the act of communicating with the dead – the Transfiguration.

There are people who absolutely blow their tops when I recount my meetings with ghosts. I seem to come across them when I take part in audience-participation radio and television programmes. They become so cross – often abusive – that I have seen some of them actually froth at the mouth when I recount how I have heard, seen or spoken to a ghost. One nonconformist minister on a radio programme the other day more or less accused me of telling untruths and of using my collar and my title of Reverend just to sell what he called my 'books of boloney ideas'. He and others declare that it is demoniac to call out the dead. I heartily agree with them. Elwyn, Winnie and I would never dream of doing this, nor would any of our medium friends. It is the dead who call us. Always, always, it is the dead who call us and not us the dead.

But the angry objectors are not content with this assurance. They shout that it is evil to have any kind of dealings with the dead. When programme interviewers ask them on what authority they say so, the answer is always the same: 'On the authority of the Bible' or, to make it even more authoritative, 'On the authority of the Word of God.' As few media studios have Bibles on hand, or the time to thumb through them searching for quotations, the matter is usually dropped, and some listeners are no doubt left believing that the Bible and the Word of God *do* forbid communicating with the dead. Listening to the radio or watching television is not like reading a book; one cannot mark one's place and check a reference to see whether what is being said is reliable or not.

There are admittedly a few references in the Bible to the wickedness of calling out the dead. The Book of Samuel speaks of the wicked witch of Endor who, for reward, called out the dead to please the living. But this is the Old Testament. What did Jesus himself say about the living communicating with the dead? The answer is that He did so Himself and enjoyed doing it. He was tired and arranged a little holiday for Himself. He decided to go to the mountain and to take His disciples Peter, James and John with Him.

> Jesus took Peter, James, and John the brother of James to a high mountain where they were alone; and in their presence he was transfigured; his face shone like the sun, and his clothes became white as the light. And they saw Moses and Elijah appear,

conversing with him. Then Peter spoke. 'Lord,' he said, 'How good it is that we are here. If you wish it I will make three shelters here, one for you, and one for Moses and one for Elijah.' Whilst he was yet speaking, a bright cloud suddenly overshadowed them and a voice called from the cloud, 'This is my son, my beloved on whom my favour rests. Listen to him.' At the sound of the voice the disciples fell on their faces in terror. Jesus then came up to them, touched them, and said 'Stand up do not be afraid.' And when they raised their eyes they saw no one but Jesus.

Matthew 17

Even the minister who accused me of telling untruths would not expect us to believe that Jesus and His disciples actually met Moses and Elijah in the flesh because we all know that they had both been dead for more than a thousand years when this meeting happened. Jesus and His disciples met the ghosts of Moses and Elijah, and it was such a wonderful experience that Peter wanted to set up three tents, one for Jesus, one for Moses and one for Elijah, so that they could all stay there longer. And all this is there to see in the Bible, the Word of God, in the Gospel according to St Matthew, chapter 17.

But what of the Afterlife itself? There is only one reference in the scriptures to Jesus speaking specifically of the place we are all destined to enter after death.

On the night before His Crucifixion, He and His disciples are together in the upper room. He is preparing these disciples, who had been His constant companions for three years, that the time had come for Him to leave them. He tells them there will be a short period when they would not see Him or converse with Him any more, as they have been used to in the past. He tells them the time has come for him to return to His father's house, and there is immediate panic. The disciples plead that they may be allowed to go with Him to this place.

Jesus then explains in simple language, without parable or

metaphor, that this is not possible. In the words of the Good News Bible, He tells them: 'Do not be worried and upset; believe in God and also in me.' And then comes this description of the place He is going to after His resurrection:

> In my father's house are many dwelling places [mansions]; if it were not so would I have told you I go to prepare a place for you? And when I go and prepare a place for you, I will come again and I will take you to myself, that where I am you may be also.
>
> John 14:1–3

One would have expected these words, spoken by Jesus on the eve of His death, to be given pride of place in the Anglican burial service. But they are not found in the 1662 Book of Common Prayer, where Job's words about 'worms destroying this his body' are given precedence. They have found their way recently into different revised versions of the Prayer Book. They occur, for example, in the Revised Burial Service of the Church in Wales, 1974. But even here they have not been given what a broadcaster would call a 'prime time slot'. According to the rubric, the words are to be used by the minister as he precedes the coffin to the churchyard or the church. More often than not they are drowned by the shuffling of pallbearers' feet and the rising of the congregation.

If Buddha had uttered similar words his monks would have embroidered them on their festal robes. Buddhists do think of the second stage of transition as a place of great bustle and activity, a place where different paths converge and different journeys are planned, a place of many dwelling places, many mansions. And nor surprisingly, the Spiritualists, who have borrowed so much of their teaching from Buddhism, Hinduism, Sufism, Rosicrucianism and other ancient religions, have pinned this particular verse to their masthead. The words 'In My Father's House are many mansions.' The stone the Anglican Church rejected, has become the cornerstone of the Spiritualist faith.

6 *Uncomfortable Words*

I am sure bishops have no idea how many people who sit in church pews Sunday by Sunday yearn to have certain questions answered. I speak from experience because, since my retirement, I have also taken my place in the pews. (And, if I may say so, it is a very uncomfortable place to be. As a priest I had plenty of leg room in the reading desk, and in the sedelia in the sanctuary, and I was well cushioned, but some of the pews must date from the times of the Inquisition.) I am convinced that if any clergyman advertised in his Parish News that he was proposing to preach on the teaching of the Church about the Afterlife, people would be prepared to walk some way to hear him – and to put up with the uncomfortable pews.

Perhaps the two most worrying questions are: 'What happens after death?' and 'Why does God allow suffering?' I am quite sure that they are closely related. It is somehow because of suffering, and the fear of suffering, in our lives that we are so anxious to know a little more about the next. So why does God allow suffering? Why did He allow the long civil war in Bosnia? Why does He allow life-threatening illnesses? Why does He allow little children to die, sometimes in great pain?

There are those who reply, 'It is not for us to know', or

'God's ways are not our ways.' But surely there *is* an answer to this, and it is to be found in the very last book of the Bible – the Book of Revelation.

> And there was war in Heaven; Michael and his angels going forth to war with the dragon. And the dragon warred and his angels and they prevailed not, neither was their place found any more in Heaven. And the great dragon was cast down, the old serpent, he that is called the Devil and Satan, the deceiver of the whole world; he was cast down to the earth and his angels were cast down with him . . .
>
> Rev 12:7–9

> He that hath understanding let him count the number of the beast; for it is the number of a man; and his number is six hundred and sixty six.
>
> Rev 13:18

Using this text, it is easy to explain the problem of suffering as follows: 'Haven't you heard, there is a war going on between God and the Devil – you can read about this bitter conflict, which began millenniums ago, in the Book of Revelation, chapter 12'. One could go on to explain how God won this first battle and how the enemy, Beelzebub, had to flee from Heaven and set up his headquarters here on earth. And because the Devil is on earth and living amongst us, the Bible warns us to be careful. 'Be sober be watchful; your adversary the devil, as a roaring lion, walketh about seeking whom he may devour' (I Peter 5:8).

St Paul also describes the enemy to us.

> For our wrestling is not against flesh and blood, but against principalities, against powers, against the world ruler of this darkness, against the spiritual hosts of wickedness in spiritual places.
>
> Eph 6:12

This war between the power of good and the power of darkness is going on around us all the time. There are many battles, and it would be foolish even to hope that God wins them all. The Devil too has his triumphs.

I remember some years ago when the film *The Exorcist* appeared in our cinemas. I had a number of young people come to see me in my office because they really had been deeply disturbed by it. Some of them had begun to believe that, like the little girl in the film, they were being possessed. My daughter Bridget was at school at the time and she decided to go and see it. I tried to dissuade her, but she insisted. She told me afterwards that she had been absolutely terrified throughout the film. The power of the Devil in the film was so overwhelming that the only way she could continue to watch it was by reminding herself that there was a God. She kept clutching herself and saying over and over again: 'Thank God there is a God. Thank God there is a God.' She had been brought up in a Christian home, and so whilst watching this fictional battle between good and evil, she was able to remind herself that whatever happened in the film, that in real life God would be the final victor.

But where there is war, there are casualties. Those of us who lived in the cities during the Second World War know all about casualties. Wave upon wave of German bombers would fly over Birmingham every night, promptly at 11 pm, and they would drop their bombs. In the morning whole streets would have been razed to the ground and there would be many dead. British soldiers at this time were fighting against German soldiers, but on the streets of Birmingham, London, Cardiff and Coventry it was old men, women and children who were being killed, maimed, blinded and crippled. They were killed not because they were bad people – good and bad people both suffered the ravages of war. The suffering had nothing whatsoever to do with being good or bad.

In the same way, cancer, Alzheimer's disease, mental and physical handicaps, war, and the death of little children are the effects of the shrapnel from the bombs of the spiritual war that is around us.

Jesus was always talking about the Kingdom of God, which could bring joy and tranquillity into our lives. But because of the continuing war, it was delayed. Jesus tells us to pray for the coming of the Kingdom: 'Thy Kingdom come. Thy will be done.' When God's Kingdom does arrive, and His will is done, the powers of darkness will have been defeated. The war will be at an end, and there will be no more casualties.

So the Devil, or the power of evil, is not to be confused with Father Christmas and the Tooth Fairy. The Devil is real and he is vicious. He is fighting to delay the Kingdom of Heaven and causing heavy casualties amongst earth-dwellers. St Paul is telling us not to stand looking up into the heavens, to stop being just a civilian spectator, to put our armour on and become active soldiers in God's army. 'Put on the whole armour of God that ye may be able to stand against the wiles of the Devil' (Eph 6:11).

Mediums and sensitives work in a number of different ways, and I have known and watched a great number of them – men and women who sit and listen to the tappings from the world beyond. These people are always very careful because they know the dangers. They are always pleased to speak to any of yesterday's people, who, for reasons of their own, decide to come back to earth life for a little frolic, or to have another look at the old place. But they are also aware of the risks involved. There is a difference – ghosts are the spirits of men and women who have crossed to the other side just a little ahead of us; an evil spirit has never been a man or a woman, and is part of that evil that had to retreat from Heaven to Earth as a result of the battle described in the Book of Revelation. Time and time again on radio and television, I have used every opportunity to warn young people, students in particular, to keep away from Ouija boards and similar gimmicks. A Ouija board is not a toy to pass away a wet evening. I know, because I have had to deal with quite a number of young people who thought otherwise.

Two terrified young women rang me on two successive nights. They did not know each other – they lived in different towns – but they had both been playing with Ouija boards, as they had many times before. On this occasion, however, they had made the wrong contact, and they were in abject terror, hardly able to speak. We said the Lord's Prayer together over and over again on the telephone, until they knew that the thing they had contacted had gone.

That is the war in Heaven. The war in the Anglican Church is quite different. It was reported in the *Sunday Express*, March, 1995 and has to do with the question of the Afterlife. It is closely linked with the war we have just been discussing.

Nearly 100 years ago, Canon Scott Holland, a canon of St Paul's Cathedral, wrote a poem about the Afterlife:

> Death is nothing at all,
> I have only slipped away into the next room.
> Call me by my own familiar name.
> Speak to me in the easy way which you always used.
> I am I, you are you;
> Whatever we were to each other that we are still.
> Put no difference in your tone.
> Wear no false air of solemnity or sorrow.
> Laugh as we always laughed at the little jokes we enjoyed together.
> Play, smile, think of me. Pray for me.
> Let my name be ever the household name that it was.
> Let it be spoken without effect, without the ghost of a shadow on it.
> Life means all that it ever meant.
> It is the same as it ever was, there is absolutely unbroken continuity.
> What is death but a negligible accident?
> Why should I be out of mind because I am out of sight?
> I am but waiting for you for an interval, somewhere very near just round the corner
> – ALL IS WELL.

It appears that many clergymen are now using this little poem in the burial service. They say it brings a great deal of comfort to the bereaved, and I am quite sure they are right; I have heard it read at several burial services recently. It is a nice enough little poem, although I must confess that if I were to hear it every Sunday at morning service it would drive me round the bend – probably because it says things that I have long since come to accept. It makes me think of Handel's Messiah. I have heard the Messiah a hundred times and every performance brings its own delight. But nothing can quite compare with the joy of hearing it for the first time. Similarly, I think, for all those people who have been brought up to believe we go off to some distant Heaven or into the fires of Hell when we die, the poem must sound like something new, exciting and full of hope.

To a family who may not have seen the inside of a place of worship in a dozen years and are now huddled together in the front seat of the crematorium chapel, the idea of Hell would be a very threatening thought, and even Heaven, with the millions of souls who have gone before, must by now be a very big and crowded place. What chance would there be of catching up with a loved one in such a place? But if he is only in the next room, as the poem says, that is marvellous.

I have stood at the reading desk in my church and at the rostrum in the crematorium, reading out the official funeral words a hundred times: 'In the midst of life we are in death; of whom may we seek for succour but of thee, O Lord, who for our sins art justly displeased', and 'Deliver us O Lord from the bitterness of eternal death.' I have now stopped wondering how the Church can expect any family which has lost a young mother, or a baby or a small child, could possibly derive a ha'pennyworth of comfort from such words. I am quite sure they do not. During these readings they seem to keep their heads down just in case they may be required to respond to any part of the service, or even join in the prayers, when they do not know how to. But when a young clergyman reads out Canon Scott Holland's little poem they seem to lift up their heads. When they go home or to the pub after the funeral, I feel sure that, if they discuss the service at all, it is the words of Scott Holland that will have stayed with them and not 'In the midst of life we are in death; of whom may we seek for succour but of thee O Lord, who for our sins art justly displeased.'

Canon Scott Holland's poem gives comfort because it is something new and exciting and full of hope, particularly to people who have no background of belief but just a vague idea of Heaven and Hell that they have picked up here or there. It must also give comfort to many regular worshippers, and even some churchwardens and members of parochial church councils, who have been nurtured from childhood on the unscriptural idea of Heaven and Hell.

But the *Sunday Express* reported that the Reverend John Cheeseman, Chairman of the Church Society, believed that the poem should not be used. The Reverend Cheeseman was reported as saying: 'The poem should not be used in funeral services because it gives false hope to the people. It is highly likely that this poem may have done people a lot of harm by inoculating them against the truth of the Gospel.' He also said: 'The poem may be nice and comforting, but it implies that in death all is well. In fact after death all may be the very opposite to well – the dead person could be on his way to hell.'

The Reverend David Streater, Director of the Church Society, used even stronger language. He said: 'It contradicts simple Christian teaching. Death is not something which is light; it should be regarded as something which is horrendous.'

If all this talk of the horrors of death is true, it makes me rather concerned about what poor 'I, Aelwyn' must be going through. It doesn't fit in at all with the vision he had of death, nor with what he learned about it from the ghosts and spirits he met. What the two clerical gentlemen are saying about death cannot possibly be true – surely Canon Scott

Holland must be much nearer the mark!

It is fair to say that he does have his backers, but they are very much a second team. The Archdeacon of York thinks all this is a lot of fuss over nothing. The Reverend Alan Drake, spokesman for the diocese of Canterbury, thinks the words are words of comfort and no more.

The canon does, however, have one great champion, more famous, more learned and perhaps more devout that even the Archdeacon of York. That champion is the very early Church father, Justin Martyr. Here I must explain that the Catholic churches have always regarded the teachings of the early fathers as second only to those of the Bible. Scholars throughout the ages have asked, 'What do the early Church fathers say?' The teachings of the fathers has always been regarded as of more authority that those of bishops or even popes, and quite naturally, the earlier the date of the person in question, the closer he would have been to the traditional teaching of Christ Himself and the more reliable his testimony. Justin Martyr is a very early father, and this is what he wrote to Trycho somewhere around the year 150: 'Those who hold that when men die their souls are at once taken up into Heaven are not to be accounted Christians or even Jews.'

So we have a choice. We can accept either the views of the Reverend Cheeseman that men and women when they die go to Heaven or to Hell, or we can accept the views of Justin Martyr, who says that this is absolute rubbish and those who propagate it are not fit to be accounted Christians or even Jews. We all know that the Anglican Church boasts of being a broad church, but surely it is not broad enough to endorse as truth the theories of both the Reverend Cheeseman and Justin Martyr, at least not without creating a considerable amount of confusion amongst its members.

And it is not just the Church of England that is having difficulty with its theory of Heaven and Hell and a spot of Paradise in between. The teaching of the Roman Catholic

Church, with the same Heaven and Hell and an even grimmer and more uninviting place in between called Purgatory, is even more confusing to its faithful.

There is no doubt that this muddled thinking on the part of the Christian churches has left the rest of us with an unhealthy fear of death and a sense of utter confusion about the Afterlife – or worse, the belief that there is no life after death. The Features Editor of the *Daily Post* told me some time ago that he had come across an opinion poll of regular church worshippers. They were asked what they believed happened after death. Over 30 per cent said they did not believe there was life after death – *and these were regular churchgoers.*

I also remember being interviewed by Vincent Kane, the toughest of Wales's television interviewers. What he wanted to make an issue of was the fact that I had said in my book *The Holy Ghostbuster*, that I did not believe in Heaven and Hell. 'You, a priest,' he said, 'say publicly that you do not believe in what the Bible says.' And this was how the interview ended, with Vincent, the educated, practising Christian, becoming very heated, because I, a parson, did not believe in Heaven and Hell. I think a good many Christians are like him; they have become so indoctrinated with the teaching of Heaven and Hell that they refuse to listen to anything different.

Even in its Decade of Evangelism, the Church prefers to let sleeping dogs lie on this piece of dogma. And if some new Christian becomes curious and decides to ask awkward questions, the Church has dozens of clichés to draw on. It talks of 'sleep' or 'Resting in the Lord' or 'Being with Jesus'. If the questioner is really strong and mature enough in the faith to take it, he will be told the whole truth, that when we die we go to a place apart. Anglicans call it Paradise, Roman Catholics call it Purgatory. It is situated halfway between Heaven and Hell. Here, in limbo, we wait for the Day of Judgement at the end of the world, when Jesus will come a second time 'to judge the quick and the dead'. We will then be told how and where to take up our final abode.

There is no suggestion that the dead in Paradise are able to make further spiritual progress. Life on earth is likened to an examination. When death comes, the heavenly invigilator tells us to put our pens down. The papers are collected and sent away to be marked, and the results come out on the dreadful Day of Judgement. But it seems that between the time when the papers are collected and the result day there is a very long waiting period – it is from the day of our death to eternity. During this time we go to sleep or enjoy 'eternal rest', and it appears to be a long, long rest.

There is, however, an explanation for this seemingly long period of waiting. I must admit that it is an explanation that gives me a great deal of comfort, but one that I have failed dismally to pass on to others from the pulpit or in confirmation classes. But I am always willing to try, so here it is.

We Earth-dwellers have a different mind/memory system from those living in the Afterlife. We can only think and rationalize in terms of past, present and future. Spirits inhabiting the Afterlife live in the Eternal Present, just as God does. Because God lives in the Eternal Present, He is able to see me at the moment of my birth and also as I lie in my coffin. There is no interval between the two sightings. For God, and for those who have passed over to the second phase, past, present and future are all one. For some reason, the earth mind has to work on three separate levels. In engineering terms, the earth mind has had a governor attached to it. A governor is something that confines or reduces the power of a machine. Governors can be fitted to the engines of vehicles to restrict their speed. Electric spanners have governors fitted to them to prevent them using too much power and wrenching the nut from the bolt. I think that the brain of the Earth-dweller has a governor fitted to it, so that it cannot see life through the wide-angled eternal present as it is viewed by those who have passed over to the other side. The result is that those who die do not have to suffer a long period of separation and grieving for their loved ones. It is only those left on earth who count the years until they are reunited.

I am quite confident that when all the paperwork has been done, all the death certificates have been signed and the vicar has found the necessary half hour to come and read the service, they will eventually take me to the crematorium. Then I can stop hovering around here, and get on with the actual crossing, so that I too will be able to enter into the Eternal Present. At this point I will need to keep my wits about me. The change from the past-present-future system to the Eternal-Present system will be even more difficult than the change we went through some years ago with metrication. But it does have its compensations. I will not have time to grieve, or to have what we Welsh people call *hiraeth* for my loved ones, because under the Eternal-Present system my loved ones will already be there with me; even my grandchildren will be around when I eventually arrive there. Their future will be my present – my 'now'. It is a peculiar idea this, and one that makes one's head hurt if one thinks about it for too long, but it is one that is full of comfort if we get used to it.

Very often when we come out with some kind of authoritative statement or statistic in conversation, we find ourselves saying, 'I just can't remember where I read that', or 'I can't remember who told me that.' Well, I am so confident about what is going to happen to me after death, and I feel so happy about the whole idea of moving from one life stage to another, a stage where I will be allowed to go on doing things, and thinking, and meeting up with loved ones, and enjoying wonderful reunions with past and present friends, and where the new life is going to be exciting once again that I don't have to think who told me about it!

I have been a priest of the Anglican Church for over 50

years, and I am ashamed to admit that I still have not the faintest idea what the Church's official teaching is about life after death, apart from it being something connected with sleep and inactivity. I learnt my comfortable words from my friends the Spiritualists.

These people boast that they possess the gift of the discerning of spirits – that great gift that the Christian churches of the world have so foolishly discarded.

By Canon Law, Anglican bishops are required to inspect all the churches in their dioceses. At these Episcopal Visitations, the churchwardens are required to present an inventory of the church's possessions, and of any gifts received during the year. But more often than not they simply open the book at the appropriate page every year and the bishop or the archdeacon will stamp 'Examined Visitation 1997' on it. If a thief had stolen anything during the year no one would be any the wiser.

The inventory of gifts I like is the one St Paul has set down in chapter 12 of his first letter to the Corinthians: 'Concerning spiritual gifts, brethren, I would not have you ignorant.' He then proceeds to list the spiritual gifts that the Holy Spirit had bestowed on the early church: 'wisdom, knowledge, faith, healing, working of miracle, prophecy, discerning of spirits, divers kinds of languages, and the interpretation of Tongues.' I suspect that past bishops have been doing the same thing to St Paul's inventory for the last 1,500 years that modern bishops are doing to parish inventories today – they have been putting a huge rubber stamp on it saying 'Examined 6th century, 7th century . . . 20th century, and found correct.' But if they had checked more carefully, they would have found that many of the gifts in St Paul's inventory have been lost to the Church over the centuries.

I am confident that the gift of wisdom is still intact. The Church very often panics and flusters, as indeed it did recently over the ordination of women, but somehow and in some peculiar way it does seem to work out all right. The gift of knowledge is still there and the Church is blessed in its leaders and scholars. I am also quite certain after 50 years in the priesthood that the gift of faith is still intact. The Church, for all its faults, has reared a good many faithful and stalwart followers of Christ. If I were Pope and believed I had the authority to canonize my fellow men, I would be able to put forward the names of a number of my clerical colleagues, and of dedicated churchwardens, church organists and lay readers.

Regrettably, however, the gift of healing has been lost for many centuries, and even in the Church of Rome it has become the last rite rather than a healing rite. But dare one hope that both the Anglican and the Roman churches are beginning to find and to pick up the bits and starting to use them once again as part of their liturgy?

The gift of prophecy, which we read about in the Old Testament and which Our Lord used so naturally in His life, is greatly frowned upon by the Church today. It is regarded as just cheap fortune telling, and our Lord's use of clairvoyance is not to be mentioned, because clairvoyance is something a gypsy does in the privacy of her own caravan – and for money. Yet I have seen clairvoyance used to help people find confidence in themselves, and to help people find the courage to think for themselves. Perhaps one day those clergymen who are picking up little bits of the gift of healing from the rubble will also find bits of the gift of prophecy and begin to use it again.

But the gift of the discerning of spirits is quite beyond the pale. In the eyes of the Church the discerning of spirits is sinful; it is something which is associated with the witch of Endor. Having said that, I must admit that when criticism has been levelled at me for having anything to do with ghosts, it has generally come from lay people, very rarely from my clerical colleagues. Successive bishops have referred people with ghost problems to me. In my younger days, I was Minor Canon of Bangor Cathedral, and my bishop was John

Charles Jones. He used to love the sessions we had in his study, when I would regale him and his wife with accounts of the things that that happened in a haunted house the previous night. I always had the feeling that Bishop John Charles would need very little persuasion to come out with me on the next one.

Other brave Anglican bishops have also appointed trained priests to tackle this problem of the discerning of spirits within their diocese, although I think it is a pity that many of these clergymen are described as 'diocesan exorcists'. The title 'diocesan exorcist' conjures up the picture of a wild-looking cleric with a 2-inch wide collar, armed with a huge crucifix, striding into a house waving and shouting for all to hear, 'In the Name of Jesus I command thee evil spirit to depart from this house.' I am quite sure that such behaviour would hurt and frighten a great number of the yesterday's people I have met and spoken to. They are not evil. All the ones I have met have been very nice people and would be very hurt to be called by anyone, least of all a clergyman, evil spirits. And as for being told to 'leave forthwith in the name of Jesus', many of them will have lived in the house much longer than the present occupant.

The Catholic churches have all lost the gift of discerning spirits. Everybody loses things from time to time, but when we do, most people make an effort to find them again. Not the churches. The churches are making no effort to find the gift of the discerning of spirits, which would bring great joy to the life of so many of their members and even if they did find it, they wouldn't know what to do with it. That is why, I think, so many good solid church members, and especially those who have suffered bereavement, can to be seen coyly wending their way to a Wednesday night seance or a Thursday night flower-healing Session at the local Spiritualist church.

7 My Friends the Spiritualists

There are two main Spiritualist organizations: the Greater World Christian Association, which has a broadly Christian basis, and the Spiritualist National Union, which does not pretend to be Christian, although I would think most of its members are Christians. My only knowledge of Spiritualism comes from the former, and it is to this organization that I shall be referring in this chapter.

It was when I was researching my book *The Holy Ghostbuster* that I began to meet, and to make friends with, members of the Spiritualist Church. I had, of course, been doing my own thing with the paranormal for many years. In the same way that learner pilots clock up flying hours, I had been clocking up hundreds of ghost-watching hours in countless haunted houses. When I decided to write a book about my experiences, I made up my mind that everything I described would be based on first-hand knowledge, not on tales that other people had told me. I went to see Winnie Marshall and gave her my car keys to hold, so that I could see for myself how she practised psychometry. I also went to her for healing, and to Bob Price's seance, during a Spiritualist service, so that I could see at first hand how they practised the gift of the discerning of spirits.

When a prominent Spiritualist told me, 'We don't have

beliefs in the Spiritualist Church – we have knowledge', she went on to explain that church members were always making contact with spirits from the beyond, and learning from them about life in its next stage. They also have the testimony of their church's pioneers, or founding fathers, men like Sir William Crookes, Sir Oliver Lodge and clergymen Stainton Moses, Maurice Elliot and Vale Owen. It appears, too, that there are spirit guides whose sole occupation it is to teach and inform those on earth what to expect in the afterlife, and how to prepare for it. It is this information, supplied by those who are living in the place itself, that enables Spiritualists to say: 'We do not believe – we know.'

So I asked my friend to share this knowledge with me. 'What do you know about the Afterlife?' I asked.

'I know that when I die,' she said, 'I will go to the Summerland. All mortals, good and bad, will go to the Summerland.'

I found the name 'Summerland' rather off-putting at first. It sounded like some amusement area in Blackpool, or the sort of place one would expect to find at the end of Brighton pier. I then tried out the name, linking it with my parents, who have been dead many years. I said to myself: 'My parents are in Paradise . . . My parents are in Hades . . . My parents are in Purgatory . . . My parents are in the Summerland.' And I liked the idea of my parents being in the Summerland. There is something warm and happy about the idea. The other day I buried a woman who was adored by her children. I was using the Anglican service: 'In the midst of life we are in death . . .' But I could not resist adding in an whisper to her grown-up children: 'Your parents are now both together again in the Summerland.'

'What about judgement in the Summerland?' I asked my friend.

'We do not believe in a final judgement at any given point in time,' she said 'Nor do we agree with the Muslim legend that there is a fine cord held over the Kedron Valley, with Mohammed holding one end of the cord and Jesus the other and that those overloaded with sin will inevitably fall into the hell fires below.'

But the Summerland does have its lower planes – the equivalent of our limbo, or Hades, to which those who have lived evil lives on earth gravitate. They are not sent there, nor are they forced to go there. It is their own nature that draws them there, where they can live out their gross desires and revel in the same selfish, evil pleasures they enjoyed when on earth, until the time comes when they eventually sicken of them and, with help, progress to a higher state.

So there is no Day of Judgement for which the faithful wait in a deep sleep. The Summerland courts of spiritual judgement are in permanent session, and each soul is his own judge and jury, often choosing corrective punishment or work to further his evolution. Some guide teachers from the Summerland also postulate that the home to which the newly arrived soul is guided is built with the material his earth sojourn provided.

To this day, I remember the tears I shed at the beginning of the autumn term when I was being transferred from the infants' class to Standard One (the first year of junior school in those days). I cried my heart out because I was due to go to Standard One the next day and I didn't know my six times table. All the new entrants to Standard One were expected to know their tables up to six. I had even heard it said that those moving to Standard Two were expected to know their twelve times table. Many a time as I have sat by the bed of a dying person as he struggled and thrashed and tore at his bedclothes, clutching at anything within reach, I have asked myself whether perhaps he too was scared of entering Standard One without having mastered his six times table in life's equivalent of infant school. But Spiritualists say there is nothing to fear. Ideally we should try and attain as high a grade of excellence as possible whilst living on earth. But for those who fail, there are second opportunity schools and nurseries available in the Summerland.

Many educationalists say, quite rightly, that it is wrong that a child's whole future should be judged on the results of one examination. But the Christian Church seems to be telling me, like an examination invigilator, that after 77 years on this earth I should now put my pen down and stop writing. Actually, having started in the infant school with a framed slate and slate pencil, I do not use a pen any more – I have just bought myself a new computer because the other was a bit too slow. So the Church is saying, 'Switch off your computer and go to sleep for a very long time, and when Judgement Day comes we will let you know whether you have passed the examination that settles your life for eternity.'

So the idea of a Summerland, where there is a great deal of activity, and where there is no time even to think about this eternal rest, attracts me. I, Aelwyn, who have lived my earth years boxed inside that old body over there, will before long have to make new decisions. I will have to choose what kind of course I wish to take in my new life, and what new skills I will have to learn. I do hope this is true.

I am also comforted to learn that most religions agree that the soul does get a little break, or a little holiday, between the two lives. Our Blessed Lord was in the grave for three days, and even after that time He still said to Mary: 'Touch me not, for I have not yet ascended to my father.' Other religions suggest an even longer rest period. Tibetan monks suggest 49 days as the period of transition.

After the break, Spiritualists tell us that we enter the kind of Afterlife described by Jesus Himself. It is the only time Our Lord describes what lies waiting for us after we die. 'In my Father's house are many dwelling places; if it were not so, would I have told you that I go to prepare a place for you?' (John 14:1–3). Anglican and Spiritualists read the same Bible, but the interpretation is different. Whereas Christian churches interpret 'many dwelling places' or 'many mansions' as referring only to three – Heaven, Hell and the place in between – to the Spiritualists the phrase means an abundance of dwelling places. The newly dead gravitate to the one of their choice, and that will be the one most like the one they had on earth. This choice of a 'dwelling place' is always linked with the ancient idea of *karma*, or reaping as one has sown.

The thing I like about the Spiritualists' belief is that it allows a choice. The newly dead are not forced to a place allocated to them; they gravitate towards the one that will suit them best. The evil man gravitates to the lower regions because he would feel happier there. In his life on earth he enjoyed lewdness and depravity, and even after death this is still what he yearns for. Similarly, others move towards the kind of life they tried to make for themselves whilst on Earth – they gravitate to their family, old friends, the kind of company they enjoyed in their earth life.

Some years ago I was invited to a conference of voluntary social workers at a rather posh hotel. I entered through the front door and walked to the main lounge, where I saw a number of men and women, all wearing conference badges, munching away at an expensive buffet lunch. It occurred to me that this kind of feast was rather unusual for a group of voluntary social workers, but I joined in and attacked the smoked salmon sandwiches with gusto. I had come to the chocolate eclair stage before commenting to the person next to me on the excellence of the meal. 'Far above what one would expect for a voluntary social worker conference,' I said.

'But my dear chap, this is not a voluntary social worker's conference,' said my companion. 'That 'do' is in the down-stairs lounge. This one is for hospital consultants.'

I very nearly choked on my cream bun. I had gravitated to the wrong 'dwelling place', and I felt most uncomfortable. I fled to my own, although in fairness, the hospital consultants who had come to know of my mistake, pressed me to stay and finish my meal with them.

Those who have visited family or friends at old people's homes and nursing homes will also appreciate this idea of gravitating. Every self-respecting home will have at least two main lounges. The large one is always the more populous. Chairs are arranged against the walls or in a wide circle, and each resident lays claim to his or her particular chair and sits on it all day long. At lunch-time the care assistant comes to wake them up and help them to the dining room. After lunch they are all escorted back again to the big lounge and once again fall easily into a semi-coma until tea-time. But visitors to the small lounge are given a very different reception. The people in this room enjoy intelligent conversation. They thirst for news of the outside world. They like to talk about the book they have just finished reading, or the clue to the *Telegraph* crossword that has baffled them because the *Telegraph* has obviously taken on a new crossword compiler, who is not half as good as the old one.

Not long ago I was summoned on the telephone by Flo Litherland, who is 98 and a founder member of the Spiritualist church in Bangor. She was one of the residents of the small lounge in our local old people's home. When I got there she introduced me to her four co-lodgers who were busy with their various activities. Then she came straight to the point and said to me quite briskly: 'I have asked you to come and see me because I wanted to ask a favour of you. When I die, will you bury me?'

I stood there for a while saying nothing, just looking at her. Then I walked slowly up to her chair and offered her my hand, and she took it. Then I said to her, 'Flo, I will bury you with the greatest of pleasure.' She gave a shriek of laughter, and her four companions also thought it was no end of a joke, me burying Flo with the greatest of pleasure! I know that my little joke has since been repeated to dozens of visitors to the small lounge.

If I should ever find myself ending my days in an old people's home, please God let me not be too senile to gravitate to the smaller lounge. There is a choice. The matron doesn't tell a new client, 'You must use the big lounge' or

'You must go to the small lounge.' Every resident makes his or her own choice and gravitates naturally to the place that pleases him or her most.

Life in the Summerland is very similar to life here on earth. There are jobs to be done, new skills to be learned and old skills to be improved. Professional people are always required. Craftsmen are always fully employed because in this new phase there are halls of learning requiring teachers. There are theatres that need actors, sportsfields that need athletes, and hospitals that need doctors and nurses. The hospitals are for those who may be in shock after the crossing over, and for those who still think they are ill and cannot get used to the idea of being free of all pain and physical illness. There are also nurseries and intensive care units in the Summerland. These are for little children who have been aborted or still-born, or who have died before they could benefit from their Earth experience. Nurses and doctors care for them, and teachers give them the instruction they failed to receive on Earth.

And the holiday that the newly dead are promised between the two phases is really not a holiday at all. It is more of a decision-making period, deciding whether to work in schools, colleges, hospitals or the theatre. Judging by the way Spiritualists describe the Summerland, there would also have to be a very big and busy jobcentre right in the middle of its High Street. Some of the job opportunities are for specialists and call for intensive training, like becoming a guide spirit who makes contact with earth mediums to teach them about the next life. Then there is a need for hordes of guardian guides to look after those of us living on earth. The Church tell us that we all have our guardian angels to care for us. Spiritualist call them guardian guides. I have never seen an angel, but I have seen a guardian guide. Elwyn has at least two. One is a Chinese gentleman with a drooping moustache and a pigtail. I have seen him. I was talking to Elwyn and looked up to see what his reaction was to something I had said, and there he was – his Chinese guide grinning at me. His other guide is a 19th-century clergyman.

It has always puzzled me, the seemingly haphazard way guides are matched to their protégées. What on earth has nonconformist Elwyn in common with a Chinese man and a 19th-century Anglican priest? Once we were in a farmhouse in Wales. The farmer was a Welshman – and a nonconformist Welshman at that. Suddenly a spirit appeared in the room and introduced himself to us as this man's guide. We talked to him and found that he had been Bishop of Bath and Wells, and that he had lived in the time of Prince Llewellyn of Wales. I will never know why a farmer in mid-Wales had been allocated a bishop, who was apparently also a nobleman, to be his guide. But that was what the person from the other side told us. I also came across a young girl of 20 who was very sensitive, with tremendous mediumistic powers, and her special guide was a priest of the Greek Orthodox Church who spoke English very haltingly.

A great number of the Summerland inhabitants choose to join the rescue service that is always searching for spirits who fail to make the crossing for some reason. The idea of rescue squads and Earth-bound spirits does rather frighten me. I have never been good at map-reading, and whenever I stop to ask people the way, they inevitably add, after giving me directions, 'You can't miss it.' But I can miss it, and I do – invariably. I find the idea that it is possible to take the wrong turning on the banks of the Jordan most disconcerting, rescue squad or no rescue squad. It does happen though, and I have experienced instances when a dead person has failed to find the entrance to the Spirit World. Having searched for some time, they return to their old haunts to carry on doing what they were doing before they died, quite unaware they are dead.

But I must emphasize that these are exceptional cases. There are not many Earth-bound ghosts, because rescue mediums on earth and those from the spirit world are always on call for this kind of accident, just as our mountain rescue groups are on the alert for accidents in Snowdonia. Most of the ghosts people see are in no way earth-bound. Many of them seem to me unusually agile. Some are just busybodies. They beg a medium on the other side to let them through, and then they beg an Earth medium to open the earth door for them. They enjoy a quick look round their old homes and perhaps a little trip, or a pilgrimage, to places where in their life they suffered traumatic emotional experiences, or where they were murdered perhaps, or where they first fell in love. Curiosity satisfied, and by courtesy of the earth medium and the spirit medium, they go back again.

Then there is the other kind of ghost, the ones who left the earth with some unresolved problem or something weighing heavily on their consciences. Some months ago a friend asked a favour of our ghost team. He had a niece whose brother had committed suicide a few months before. The brother had been a dentist, and his business had been a flourishing one. He was very happily married; he had a wife who worshipped him and three lovely small children. He had everything going for him and yet one Saturday afternoon he drove himself to a quiet spot out of town and injected himself with sufficient poison to kill a horse. It was a mystery to his family and to the coroner why he should have wanted to put an end to his life. But he had; there was no question about that.

His sister was convinced that he was now in the house where she lived with her husband and children. She was not afraid, and she explained that she wanted our help more for him than for herself and her family. Little did she realize, when she invited us, that her house was full of ghosts. There were ghosts in that house from practically every generation. There were some even from the Middle Ages, and they were all queuing for Elwyn to give them the final assistance they needed so that they could join us in the front parlour for a chat. Elwyn helped several of them over and we talked to them. Nothing of any great importance emerged; one of them told us about his farm and another told us how well her children were doing at school. But there was no sign of the brother who had committed suicide.

So we had a break and a cup of tea and Elwyn tried again. After a bit, he said, 'I can see him – or I think I can. He is standing in the shadows and he is reluctant to come forward.'

'We are here to help you,' he said to him. 'Come and join us. We all want to help you.'

'He is holding something in his hand,' Elwyn told us, and then he said: 'It is a photograph of a very nice-looking young girl in her teens, or early twenties. Now,' he continued 'he has turned his back on us, and he is walking away from us very slowly.'

After another break and another trawl in the unseen, Elwyn saw him again. But he refused to come near enough for the rest of us to see him. 'He is sitting by a dark rock,' Elwyn said. 'His knees are doubled up under his chin and I think he is crying. Talk to him, Aelwyn!'

'Tell me why you are sad,' I said.

'He is sad because he is lonely,' Elwyn answered for him.

'But,' I said, 'there's no need for you to be lonely. Your sister is here with us and she tells me that you have both your father and mother on your side with you. And she tells me too that you were always your grandmother's blue-eyed boy. Why don't you go and hunt up your parents and your grandma? They will help you.'

Then Elwyn replied for him again: 'He says he can't do that because he is ashamed of what he has done.'

We did not ask whether he was ashamed of the way he had let his little family down by committing suicide, or whether the shame was connected in some way with the photograph he had shown us of the attractive young lady in her early twenties. But the spirit telegraph system on the other side works faster than any 999 calls. A male relative appeared and assured us it would be all right. 'Leave it with me,' he said. 'I'll see what can be done.'

One cannot check on every visit one makes, but it is now over a year since we were in that house and we have had no request for a return visit.

If someone asked me what my work was before I retired I would say that I worked as a church social worker with drug addicts and alcoholics. But it would be equally true to say that I was a social worker and counsellor to a good number of ghost clients. I found that many of them just wanted the chance to explain their innocence to some earth person, or to say they were sorry for something they had done. After that they would return to their own domain never to return again.

Knowing Winnie Marshall has given me quite an insight into this crossing of the chasm. Winnie lost her son Christopher in an accident many years ago. He was 21 when he died. But she told me he is always pottering around the house and she never grieved for him after he was dead because he was in the house with her even when she was making the arrangements for his funeral. 'I see far more of him now that he is dead than I would have if he had lived and gone to work in Aberdeen,' she told me. And of course Christopher is the lucky one. He has only to persuade the guardian at the Summerland end to let him through to earth life, because his mother is one of the Earth-door guardians. She always leaves the door 'on the latch' for her Christopher.

It is tempting to ask: 'If people have tasks to carry out in the Summerland, how is it this young man is able to spend so much time in his mother's house in Colwyn Bay?' The answer is, of course, that ghosts are omnipresent; they can be present in several places at the same time. They can journey into the future or the past at will, or even visit the three time stages all at the same time. It seems that we Earth-dwellers are greatly handicapped by having to carry around these clumsy carnal bodies of ours!

So we have this Afterlife place that is warm and summery, a

place where there is a choice of many dwellings and a choice
of different kinds of work to do and the skills required to do
them. There is even, apparently, the choice of whether to stay
close to base or to take little journeys from time to time to
see how things are going on in the old places on Earth.

As Earth-dwellers, our great boast is that God has given us
free will. God does not force us to be good. We are allowed
to choose between good and evil. At the time of
confirmation, children take upon themselves the promises
made for them at their baptism, promising to renounce the
Devil and all his works. Nobody forces them to do this.
Born-again Christians tell us the hour and the day they gave
themselves to Christ; it is always their own decision – there
is no compulsion. We also know that, in exercising this free
will, there are probably some people who choose to worship
the Devil. Clergymen have always had to guard against these
devil worshippers and see to it that the aumbry, the little wall
safe that houses the reserved sacrament, is carefully locked so
that no one can take away the consecrated bread and carry it
away for use in Devil-worship.

Earth life offers limitless choice, but it has always puzzled
me that, if we are Christians, it seems that the moment we
die, the freedom of choice is completely extinguished. We are
taught that at death we are all met at the Golden Gate. We
are then directed to Paradise or a place of waiting. We are
given the command to go to sleep or to 'receive eternal rest'.
We are so brainwashed that we begin to think that this
resting, this sleeping until eternity, is good for us. We express
it as a hope and as a prayer on the tombstones of our dear
ones: 'Rest eternal grant to him, O Lord', or 'May he rest in
peace', or just 'RIP'.

If we did a survey in our high streets and asked people
'What do you think of the Church's teaching that when we
die, we go to sleep until the day of judgement?', I am sure
most people would want to say, 'It gives me the bloody
creeps.' Ask about the Summerland, however, and I think the

reply would be different. The idea of being active again, being able to choose again and able to make a fresh start again – that is marvellous!

There is a saying, 'Not only must justice be done, it must be seen to be done.' It is surely also fair to say, 'Not only must the Church's beliefs be reasonable, they must be seen to be reasonable.'

Whether the teaching of the Spiritualist Church is true or false I cannot judge. But I do know that all my Spiritualist friends are nice people to know. I also find Quakers very nice people to know. This to me has always been a variant of the 'hen or the egg' question. Are they nice because only nice people join the Spiritualist and the Quaker religions? Or is it that these religions create nice people?

My work with alcoholics makes me think the latter. Possibly the finest, kindest and most tolerant people I know are the reclaimed alcoholics I have worked with. These are men and women who, when drinking alcohol, suffer a chemical change in their bodies, which in turn creates an uncontrollable craving for drink which non-sufferers can never comprehend. This craving drags them into the depths of misery and degradation. Everything they previously loved is taken away from them. They lose their work and family and friends turn their backs, but at the time it matters not a damn. All that matters is the wherewithal to buy drink tomorrow. They don't eat, they don't wash, and they smell. They cultivate a charm known only to the alcoholic; they make promises which they break. They tell lies. They become people who are very difficult to love or even to help.

Experts say that the fall from man to flotsam takes in the region of ten years. If at the end of this period they ask for help, there is always ready, in every town, and now very often in villages, that most wonderful organization Alcoholics Anonymous waiting for their call. A brother is sent to bring them into that circle where all are under the same curse. They help each other to fight this craving from

Hell. The new member will be allocated a guardian who can be called whenever the tremors become unbearable. Other members of AA will ferry him to programmed sessions in neighbouring towns because they know he needs more support than their weekly meeting can offer. He is made to eat and to meet people again. Clean clothes are given and a great deal of love and care. And if he falls flat on his face time and time again, the brethen are always there to pick him up, because they also fell flat on their faces time and time again when they first called for help. Every single member of AA, even the leaders and guardians, remind themselves daily that they are alcoholics. When they introduce themselves at a meeting they will say: 'I am Bill and I am an alcoholic. I haven't had a drink for five years' five months' two weeks and three days, but I don't know what tomorrow will bring.' These people, the prosperous-looking business people who have been able to reclaim their lives, and the shivering, tattered people who have still not recovered from the effects of meths, meet together to help each other.

I have often been a guest at open meetings of AA. The last time an invitation came, I was told I could bring a friend with me and I invited my bishop. The meeting was in Holyhead. On the way there in the car I explained the set-up to the bishop; I told him that this was an open meeting and that the regular members would have been told of our coming and given the choice of whether to attend or not. So it was quite possible his doctor, his bank manager and one or two members of his cathedral chapter would choose to stay home that night. We could, however, expect to see about 20 regular AA members and a similar number of guests. I tried to explain to him how to tell the difference between members and non-members. 'Look out for the really expensively dressed men and women,' I told him. 'Most of the guests, like you and me, will be wearing off-the-peg suits. But the reclaimed alcoholic, as if rebelling against the day when he was filthy and smelly and covered in his own vomit, will be dressed in a designer suit; I also told the bishop to be on the lookout for the men and women who spoke to him in a soft, quiet voice. The likelihood would be that they too would be alcoholics. The low, quiet speaking would be their reaction against the raving and shouting of drunken days.

Three speakers mounted the rostrum that night. One after the other told the audience how low they had sunk before asking for help. Nothing was left to the imagination. Then came talk of their progress, of the fight back to normality, talk of finding new jobs, of reconciliation with their families, of finding new friends, and then at the end: 'And did you see that new red Jaguar in the car park as you came in? Well that's mine.'

This was followed by a roar of cheering and foot-stamping from the members. They all felt pleased for him, and they all hoped fervently that they would be given the strength from some higher being to follow him and one day possess their own red Jaguar.

When we came out of the meeting, the bishop said: 'I'm sorry I didn't take your tip and sit in the front. I couldn't hear all that was being said, sitting in the back. But,' he added, 'I could feel a power of love filling that room tonight.' I ventured to say that I thought the upper room at Pentecost must have felt a bit like the room we were in, only they had flames of fire and we had incessant cups of tea.

I have often reminded my little congregation in St Tegai's (poor things) of the atmosphere of love I always felt at AA meetings, and suggested that we should all try to generate the same kind of love-power in our church. One of the rebuked, bless him, did ask me how I thought this love was initiated. I think it is the same love, the same kindredship, the same companionship, that was found in the bomb shelters during the war – people banding together to fight the same common enemy. I think that it also has a lot to do with AA's teaching, as embodied in its Twelve Steps. These people have, during their worst years, brought a great deal of pain and suffering to their spouses, their families and their friends. They have cheated and lied and brought misery to all who cared for them. But in the AA meetings where these former cheats and liars were congregated, there was this great warmth of love. I can only suggest that the one thing these people have in their meetings that we do not in our churches is the Twelve Steps. What a wonderful thing it would be if the church, in its Decade of Evangelism, borrowed AA's Twelve Steps!

When an alcoholic attends his first meeting, he is told quite categorically that AA is not a religious organization, and then he is asked almost immediately, 'Do you believe that a power greater than yourself can restore you to sanity?' He is then presented with a copy of the Twelve Steps. These are the suggested stages through which an estimated 2,000,000 men and women across the world have achieved sobriety in the fellowship of Alcoholics Anonymous.

I wonder what would happen if, at the beginning of Lent, the same Twelve Steps were presented to every worshipping Christian, and we each substituted our own besetting sin or impediment for the word 'alcohol' – envy, resentment, pride or whatever. Would it help a couple of million of us to achieve some degree of sanctity?

The Twelve Steps of Alcoholics Anonymous

1   We admitted we were powerless over alcohol – that our lives had become unmanageable.
2   We came to believe that a power greater than ourselves could restore our sanity.
3   We made a decision to turn our will and our lives over to the care of God *as we understood Him.*
4   We made a searching and fearless moral inventory of ourselves.
5   We admitted to God, to ourselves and to another human being, the exact nature of our wrongs.
6   We were entirely ready to have God remove all these defects of character.

7   We humbly asked Him to remove all our shortcomings.

8   We made a list of all persons we had harmed and became willing to make amends to them all.

9   We made direct amends to such people whenever possible, except when to do so would injure them or others.

10   We continued to make personal inventory and when we were wrong promptly admitted it.

11   We sought through prayer and meditation to improve our conscious contact with God, *as we understood Him*, praying only for knowledge of His will for us and the power to carry that out.

12   Having had a spiritual awakening as a result of these steps, we tried to carry this message to alcoholics and to practise these principles in our affairs.*

AA meetings worldwide close with this prayer, which I will use to close this chapter:

> Lord, grant me the serenity to accept
> the things I cannot change,
> The courage to change the things I can,
> And the wisdom to know the difference.

*The Twelve Steps are reprinted with permission of Alcoholics Anonymous World Services, Inc. Permission to reprint the Twelve Steps does not mean that AA has reviewed or approved the contents of this publication, nor that AA agrees with the views expressed herein. AA is a program of recovery from alcoholism *only* – use of the Twelve Steps in connection with programs and activities which are patterned after AA, but which address other problems, or in any other non-AA context, does not imply otherwise.

8 Mourning the Dead

Meanwhile back at the vicarage in Llandegai, I am almost certain I heard the woman crouching here behind the sofa with me telling her friend that the house seemed rather quiet. If she is insinuating this is because nobody in the house is missing me or grieving for me, I can tell her categorically she is wrong – quite wrong. I have a wife, six children and 17 grandchildren, and I used to get on very well with them all. I know they grieve for me. The fact that they are not making a big show of their affection and having hysterics over my coffin doesn't mean they don't care. Grieving and mourning the dead takes many different forms.

I remember in the late 1960s listening to Dr W Dewi Rees, who at that time was a doctor in Llanidloes, Mid-Wales, delivering a fascinating lecture on the discipline of mourning the dead. Over the years he has carried out valuable research into this subject. He found that there were not only the expected psychological problems of withdrawal and depression, there was also a catalogue of other physical ailments following in the wake of a bereavement. Widows and widowers became more prone to heart attacks than their married contemporaries and bachelors. This was a phenomenon that occurred worldwide.

Dr Rees wrote:

Widowed people commonly show signs of increased ill health. Twenty-one per cent of widows in Boston, USA, 32 per cent in Sydney, Australia and 43 per cent of London widows reported a deterioration in their health during the 13 months following a bereavement. Medical consultations were also found to have increased by 63 per cent in London widows during the six months following a bereavement . . .

There are good reasons for supposing that a person's immune system may be impaired by grief. One study of the bereaved looked at blood lymphocyte response to mitogen in widows.

Another comparative study showed a lowering of the NK (natural killer) cells' activity in recently bereaved spouses. Dr Rees suggests in his thesis 'The Hallucinatory Reactions of Bereavement':

1 The stress of bereavement produces an increase in ACTH from the pituitary gland.
2 The ACTH stimulates the adrenal cortex to release or to activate corticoteroide.
3 The corticoteroide depresses the mechanism of the body.

As you can see it is written in 'Medicalalese' for the understanding of other doctors, but I think Dr Rees is saying that people who have suffered a bereavement very often, but not always, have a need to see a doctor more often that before, in the case of London widows, 43 per cent reported a worsening of their health following a bereavement.

He is also saying that people who have suffered a bereavement should not ignore these new illnesses. They are real, because during the stress of mourning the death of a dear one, a person's immune system is often weakened, and the bereaved is susceptible to any illness that is going around.

Dr Rees also says something else I find most interesting. He tells the bereaved that there are two places where they should look for help: the doctor's surgery and the community where they live. He says:

This does not mean that the treatment is the concern primarily of doctors and nurses and that it is best treated with drugs, though at times these can be helpful. But other people have to be involved, and other forms of support provided, of which the most important is social support.

What I find interesting is that he is not suggesting the bereaved should see a counsellor – that modern panacea for all ailments. I think he is recommending good old-fashioned common or garden neighbourhood help.

I am amazed how much research has gone into the subject of bereavement; and other researchers have also stressed the need for community help. So, what is this help, and where can it be found? Do we look for it in the town or in the country? Let us see. Mary and Bill had moved into a fifth-floor flat in Birmingham. They both went out to work and saw very little, if anything, of their neighbours. One morning, on his way to the office, Bill was involved in an accident and killed. A policeman called at the flat and broke the news to Mary. Later she accompanied him to the mortuary to identify the body. The policeman was very kind. The hospital authorities were also concerned, and they gave her the name and telephone number of an undertaker, who called to see her at the flat. He was very efficient and businesslike, and took over all the arrangements. Later he phoned to tell her that the only slot he had been offered at the local crematorium was at 9.20 am on Thursday morning. If she could be there by 9 o'clock, he would meet her there. Oh, and by the way, did she want a Church of England or nonconformist funeral? The crematorium would provide a rota minister, provided they knew which denomination she wanted.

Now let us look at a rural example. Tom and Ann had a smallholding in Aberdesach. Ann worked part-time in Caernarfon. When she left for work, Tom was already out on the tractor ploughing the Rectory field. Later that morning the rector called at her office to break the news that Tom had

had an awful accident with the tractor and had been rushed to Gwynedd Hospital, and offered to drive her there. When they arrived, the sister at the accident ward told Ann there was nothing they could have done – Tom was dead on admission.

The Birmingham community would not know of Bill's death; they would not even know who he was. But everyone in the village of Aberdesach would know of Tom's dreadful accident within minutes. Ann would have been brought home by the rector and in no time a self-appointed friend or neighbour would have taken charge of her house of mourning. How the 'Bereavement Companion' is appointed from amongst the new widow's friends and neighbours has always been a great mystery to me. Where she graduated to carry out the work is an even greater mystery. Being a bereavement companion requires a great deal of complex generic knowledge.

In the days before the war, the protocol was strict. The curtains of the house of mourning were tightly drawn. Those of neighbouring houses were drawn to a degree dictated by their nearness to the house of mourning, after due consultation with the bereavement companion. On the first evening after the death, when the men had come from work, the neighbours would begin to call to offer their condolences. It was at this stage that the bereavement companion began to ply her trade. When the first couple arrived the companion would open the front door for them and usher them into the presence of the widow in the front parlour. Here Ann would tell her first visitors how it had all happened.

'Tom got up very early because he wanted to plough the Rectory field. When I left for work I honked my car horn and waved to him, and he, bless him, threw me a kiss. The next think I knew was the rector coming to the office with the manager and telling me that Tom had had an accident. When we got to the hospital the ward sister was very kind and she told me there was nothing they could have done, because

Tom was dead before the ambulance arrived.'

At this stage the handkerchief would come out, Ann would have a little cry and a sniffle, and it would be the neighbours' turn to express their sorrow. 'You know if there's anything we can do, you've only to ask. You know where to find us.' Then they would instinctively find their way out through the back door.

Whilst this was going on in the front parlour the companion would have opened the front door to the second couple. She would delay their entrance to the front parlour by discussing the awfulness of the tragedy and the shock, and by imparting little snippets of information about how it happened. And all the time keeping her ear glued to what was happening in the front parlour. Then suddenly she would announce: 'I think you can go in now.' As the back door closed quietly behind the first visitors, the second couple would be ushered into the parlour so that Ann could once again relate how it all had happened.

And so the community therapy would continue. In that darkened room, Ann would have told the story of how Tom died many times before the funeral. Tom was dead. It was no dream. She would have to get used to it.

During the funeral service the grieving would continue. Some of the nonconformist ministers were expert bereavement therapists. The official counsellor, Miss Myfanwy Jones, BSc (1st Class Hons, Sociology) would be considered an ignoramus in the art of bereavement therapy by all those who had known the ways of the Reverend Elias Wynne, BA, BD.

Ann's mother would have confided in the Reverend Wynne that although Ann had had many callers the shock had not yet come out. She had not had what one would call a 'real cry'. The Reverend Wynne would have nodded and said, 'Leave it with me; I will see to it.' During the extempore prayer at the funeral service he would ask his Heavenly Father to visit Rose Cottage Farm where He would find Ann with her little heart broken, desperately lonely without the companionship of Tom, that wonderful man who had adored her. Long before he had finished his homely conversation with his Heavenly Father, Ann would be in floods of tears.

The undertaker would be Mr Hughes Halfway House. 'Halfway House' was a necessary part of his title. It was where he lived, and it served to mark him out from all the other Mr Hugheses in the parish. He could have been known as Mr Hughes the Coffin, but as there were two other undertakers in the area called Hughes this would not have been very practical. Mr Hughes Halfway House would be surveying the scene from the back of the church and he would smile and nod. Yes, you could always rely on the Reverend Wynne.

But the undertaker would know that at the end of the service in the churchyard, it would be his responsibility to continue the therapy. During the singing of the last hymn in the churchyard, he would take his place at the side of the grave. From this vantage point he would invite, or instruct, the members of the family to join him, one at a time, in strict protocol, on the wooden framing of the grave. One hand would hold the hand of the mourner and the other would be on the nape of her neck, so that if necessary, he could bend her head forward to peer at the coffin in the grave for the last time. One looked and one wept – that was the procedure.

This kind of therapy is no longer available in the twenty-minute burial sessions at crematoria today. I find that when young undertakers timidly ask members of the family if they wish to see the coffin while it is still on the catafalque and before it passes from the chapel, about half will say yes, and half will decline. Mr Hughes Halfway House would not have approved of that.

I would suggest that the bereaved people therapeutically treated by the Reverend Elias Wynne BA, BD and his colleague Mr Hughes Halfway House, would not have as much ACTH produced in their pituitary glands to activate corticopteroide as others. I would also think that the rural bereaved would return to work, and to a normal life, much sooner than their urban compatriots.

As a retired parish priest, I say without malice or prejudice that it was a sad day for the country when it decided to sack its ministers and priests and appoint in their place a monster Social Services Department of professional carers and counsellors in every town or county hall in the land. The social workers of today aim to give families what they call 'support'. They visit and they give advice and encouragement. But in the poverty days of 50 years ago this would not have been sufficient. It was often money, cash in hand, that people needed.

I remember when I was eight years of age going to the corner shop on some errand for my mother and stopping to see a multitude of people standing in the road opposite a small terraced house. In a way that only a child can, I pushed myself to the front of the crowd and peered over the fence into the little front garden. There on the top step a coffin had been placed to rest on two kitchen chairs, and on the coffin was a basin of water. Behind the coffin stood the Reverend Elias Wynne. He still had his hat on his head because he had not yet called the people to pray with him. He was looking over the heads of a vast crowd of quarrymen, all dressed in their Sunday best suits and bowler hats, milling around uneasily below him and speaking in whispers. Standing one on each side of the Reverend Wynne were two children, a boy of about 11 and a little girl who was in my class. The little girl was standing next to a man dressed in black and holding his hand. Everyone seemed to be waiting for something.

Suddenly it happened. There was a 'whoosh' from the crowd, just like the sound one hears on the football field when the ball scrapes over the goal post but more restrained. At the same time, a lady with white hair, dressed in a black satin dress and wearing a bonnet with black flowers woven into it, came out of the house. She was carrying a little baby wrapped in a white shawl. The lady came and stood near the Reverend. He took off his hat and placed it on the windowsill. He then took the baby from the lady and held it in his arms. Then in a loud voice he cried out: 'Let us pray.' The quarrymen all around the house took off their bowler hats and everything was quiet. Then the minister said: 'We baptise this child Mary Elizabeth. In the name of the Father and of the Son and of the Holy Ghost, Amen.' And then he went on to say 'Grant, O Lord, that this child may die unto sin.' At these words, he placed the little baby on the lid of the coffin and all the men said, 'Amen.' Then the Reverend lifted the baby into the air again and with a loud voice said: 'So that she may live unto righteousness.' And all the people shouted 'Amen' and and 'Praise be to God'.

When the old lady in black had taken the baby back to the house the minister spoke to the people. It was the first time in my life I saw grown men crying. Some kept their heads down, others were blowing their noses on their red spotted handkerchiefs. But some were crying out loud as children do in school. Then there was a collection. Men in different parts of the crowd held their hats and collected money in them from the other men. When the hats were full, they took them to the Reverend Wynne, and he placed them on the coffin and prayed again for a very long time.

It was some years before I realized the significance of what I had seen. I had apparently witnessed a coffin-lid baptism. It was the baby's mother, who had died in childbirth, who was being buried, and it was the baby's father and brother and sister who were standing behind the coffin during the ceremony.

And the collection? I was told years later that the Reverend Wynne would have considered himself to have performed badly if a coffin-lid collection for the widower and his children had failed to reach the equivalent of £1,000 in today's money. It was highly likely, too, that the quarrymen would arrange a charity concert for the family before the end of the year.

In the days before the war, all who called at a house of mourning would discreetly leave money in the front parlour. It was a stipulated amount – half a crown. A worker's pay in those days was £2 per week, so half a crown was one sixteenth of a week's wage – say £10 in today's money. It didn't savour of charity; it would be given to everyone, including the doctor's widow, the bank manager's widow – there was no means test. Only the one question was asked: 'It is to be a public funeral?' If so, one took one's half crown, and left it in the parlour when one went to condone. Most villages in Wales could boast, in the years before the war, that a funeral would have been paid for by the community before the hearse left the front door.

This may have been the kind of community care Dr Dewi Rees was thinking of. Today things are different. 'The Church has a ministry of burial for the dead,' one colleague said to me, 'but it no longer has a ministry of mourning for the bereaved.' I am sure he is right. We still have our occasional and very special Reverend Wynnes, those masters of pastoralia. But as a body and as a caring organization, the Church has little to offer the bereaved. These people may be in danger of suffering physical and psychological illnesses, but orthodox religion seems to have little to offer except the hackneyed palliatives: 'Time is a great healer,' 'God the Holy Spirit will give you a very special healing balm.'

Church members know this. They know instinctively that the Church has no equipment or knowledge to deal with the problems of bereavement. Centuries ago it lost the gift of the discerning of spirits that the Early Church so treasured, and with this loss it also lost its understanding of death and what happens after death. Ghosts, and those people who say they have dealing with ghosts, are regarded as peculiar and cranky by many of today's clergy.

Dr Rees also researched what some would call the paranormal effects on people suffering bereavement. He called this study 'A Longitudinal Survey of The

Consequences of Bereavement'. He prepared a list of 26 factors to discuss with bereaved relatives. He says:

> After commencing a pilot study, in which the patients invariably proved helpful, I was impressed by the extent to which people talked of their hallucinatory experiences of the dead and of experiencing a sense of the presence of the dead person.

The survey, as one would expect, was run on a strictly scientific basis. Dreams were noted when mentioned, but these were carefully differentiated from hallucinatory experiences which occurred in full consciousness, and were not included in the final analysis. Experiences which occurred at night, other than those occurring immediately after retiring to bed, were discounted as dreams. Indeed, if there was any doubt about the reality of any experience a nil response was recorded.

The great surprise of the survey was that almost half the widowed people interviewed reported having seen, having been spoken to, or having been touched by a departed partner on many occasions. I have Dr Rees' permission to relate some of the testimonies he had from some 258 widowed people he visited during the time it took to complete the survey. The figures in brackets are the duration of widowhood.

> It is a sacred thing. I feel there is some nearness, he hasn't actually gone out of my life. I am never afraid. (3½ years)

> He seems so close. (7 years)

> Very often he is by my side. It's a funny thing, but I have never dreamed of him. (7 years)

> I feel he is watching me. (2 years)

> He is here now. I am not a bit nervous or miserable. Whenever I go out, I always want to return home because he is there. I slept from the first night he was buried. (8 years)

> There is nothing like it. It is worth all the money in the world to

me. It's a lovely feeling. I am very happy and I never feel alone.
(10 years)

I felt for about a week, two years ago, that he was with me all the time. I was not afraid of it. (10 years)

I feel that he is with me and looking after me. Before he died I was always terrified of going upstairs, and wouldn't go without a light. Since he died I don't mind going upstairs one little bit.
(11 years)

If something crops up, I feel him very close and I am guided by him. (3 years)

I fancy if I left here I would be running away from him. Lots of people wanted me to leave, but I couldn't. I often hear him walking about. He speaks quite plainly. He looks younger, and as he was when he was all right, never as he was when he was ill. (9 months)

The report says: 'Most of the people interviewed (69 per cent) found perceptions of the dead helpful and only a small proportion (6 per cent) found them unpleasant.' And Dr Rees gives examples of those who thought the experience unpleasant:

I felt him touch me. It frightened me. It made one think you were going up the wall. (8 years)

When I heard his voice I would think, why, he's alive, and then would think, no, he can't be, he is dead. It upset me very much. It wasn't right. (4 years)

I was able to tell Dr Rees that the lady who though it 'wasn't right' reminded me of one of my call-outs. I was asked by a psychiatric nurse if I would visit a patient of hers who had been suffering from the most awful depression. She was the young mother of two small children and her husband had been killed in an accident. But he still came back. She could feel him sitting on her bed at night; she even knew whether he approved or disapproved of the things she had been doing during the day. She hated it so much that she moved house so that she could get away from him, but he followed her to the new address. She told me: 'When that man was alive I loved him more that I had loved anything in my life. But he is dead now and he is making me neither wife nor widow. He should leave us alone now. Somebody should tell him he is dead and we are alive.' The young widow had kept the secret of her haunting husband to herself. The bitterness of her status – married yet not married – had been burning inside her for a couple of years and her depression had come very near to a point of no return. She had told no one, not the doctor or the nurse who had been so kind to her, not even her mother. She had lost her appetite, and she very nearly lost her life because of the awful sessions she was having with her dead husband.

Elwyn came to the rescue. He gave the young widow a choice. He told her that her husband probably wanted to tell her something and was unable to make her hear him. 'He is here now,' he said.

'Yes, I know. I can feel he's standing there by the kitchen door,' she replied.

'You have a choice,' said Elwyn. 'I think I can make it possible for him to talk into my mind and I can tell you what he is saying. Or else, if you let me help you relax a little and go into a very light trance, you will be able to hear him yourself and perhaps even talk to him.'

'I'll hear him for myself.' she said.

And so it happened. It seemed that his death had not been an accident; it had been suicide. The minute he was dead he had regretted this cowardly act, which had brought so much sorrow to her and the children. He wanted to tell her that he was sorry. During that conversation, they also in some way came to an agreement that there would be no need for further chats, that henceforth he would stay on his side of the fence and she on hers. That afternoon I saw the depression of years, which had made a young girl look, feel and act like a tired old woman, disappear in minutes.

It surprised me that this young women could have suffered so much without saying a word about her husband's visitations to anyone else. Dr Rees came across similar reluctance in his research. Of his interviewees, 72.3 per cent had not mentioned their experience to anyone else, and those who had, had usually told a friend outside the family. None had informed their doctor and only one person out of the 258 people interviewed had confided in a minister of religion.

Reading Dr Rees's report left me in no doubt that his main purpose was to gain the extra knowledge that would enable him and others to improve methods of treating the bereaved. But the very logical sub-conclusion he comes to at the end of his report is something every thinking Christian person, and certainly every minister of religion, should consider very, very carefully.

> The Christian belief in the Resurrection of Christ is based on the reports of the disciples who met Jesus after his Crucifixion Similar phenomena are experienced, in a lesser way, by millions of people today. If the Resurrection of Jesus is true, then the perceptions of the dead by widowed people living today must be accorded their own, albeit less significant, reality. It is illogical to accept the one and deny the other, especially as the bereaved report, just like the disciples, that they have heard, spoken to and been touched by the deceased. This is obviously a difficult issue for the Church to resolve and one can understand the reluctance Christian leaders may have in approaching it. Nevertheless it is a subject which needs to be widely discussed . . . A theology of the Resurrection must remain incomplete if the current experiences of the widowed are not somehow incorporated in it. One cannot say that Christ lives, and that this fact was proven by his Reappearance 2,000 years ago, but that the perceptions of the dead experienced by many people today have no reality.

9   *Reincarnation*

—

I don't think I have ever experienced a fear of death. Until quite recently, I don't think I have even actually given the subject a great deal of thought. It was when I started the silly practice of reading obituaries in my local paper that the awful truth began to dawn: 'The days of our years are three score years and ten.'

Some of my friends were only just beginning to enjoy a little discount when their names began to appear in the obituary columns. But although reading obituaries failed to instil in me a fear of death, they did set me thinking about the *manner* of my death. Obituary notices not only give information about the funeral arrangements, they also indicate the cause of death. Donations in aid of cancer research or some other medical cause tell their own tale. Donations in aid of the parish church usually suggest a quiet, peaceful death in bed at home.

I became anxious about the kind of death that would require me to sit in a chair for years speechless, paralysed down one side of my body, frustrated and bad tempered because I couldn't make people understand what I was saying. I also became worried about any kind of illness that would compel me to consume drugs to kill the pain in my body. I became alarmed at illnesses that take away a person's dignity – Alzheimer's disease, CJD and many others. And I also became afraid of dying in a hospital ward where teenage nurses called me 'Grandpa'.

As a clergyman I must have said or sung that beautiful little service called the Litany hundreds of times, and said: 'Good Lord deliver us from lightning and tempest, from plague, pestilence and famine, from battle and murder and from sudden death.' I ask myself now whatever possessed me, in those far-off days, to pray, and to encourage my congregation to pray, that we might all be delivered from sudden death.

I used to think of death as something new and exciting, some kind of new adventure. But now that I have made myself dead for the last three days, I am even becoming afraid of death itself. Last week someone told me that three-quarters of the population of the world believe in reincarnation. He added: 'And if 75 per cent of the population of the world believes in this kind of life after death, there must be something in it.' I thought that the 25 per cent who did not believe in it would be the people of the Western world – Christians and Jews in Europe and America, and also possibly Muslims in the Middle East. It was a comfort to know that my own people supported me in my antipathy towards reincarnation. It was then that another friend told me that a Sunday newspaper had run a poll asking whether readers believed in Heaven and Hell, or whether they believed we live another life on earth. Half voted for Heaven and Hell, and half for reincarnation.

I was amazed. I have never read the same book twice, nor watched a film or television programme a second time. I love the Greek Islands, but I would never revisit the same island. So the man who has been dead three days is now terribly afraid of what is to happen to him. What if after all the looking forward, all the hassle of the funeral service and everything that goes with it, I am merely to do a U-turn and come back again to this same old earth as a baby boy or girl – reincarnation is apparently no respecter of the sexes.

I had a very happy childhood. My wife and I were blessed with six wonderful children and the number of our grandchildren multiplied to 17. The Church was also good to me. It trusted me with the work of placing children for adoption, and later with work with alcoholics and drug addicts – all good, challenging jobs. We had a lovely house and a beautiful garden. It has been a good life. Whenever I think of our family, I always think with gratitude of the wonderful new translation of the Lord's Prayer in the New English Bible: 'Deliver us not into the test', and in the Good News Bible: 'Do not bring us to the hard testing.' These words make so much more sense than the Authorized Version: 'And lead us not into temptation' and describe so well the kind of life my family and I have been allowed to lead. Up to the time of my death, neither I nor any member of my family has been called upon to undergo 'the test' or 'the hard testing'. Not one of us has had to face great sorrow or illness. God has been good to us, but for all that, I would hate having to come back to live another life, in another body, on this earth. I would not even want to come back as the Archbishop of Canterbury – perhaps especially not as the Archbishop of Canterbury!

As I think of reincarnation, I also keep thinking of Esther Rantzen, that good lady who has set up a telephone helpline for children who are being shamefully abused, often by their own parents and grandparents. Does *karma* ('reap as you have sown'), the belief that seems so closely linked with the idea of reincarnation, mean that if I have not pulled my weight in this life, I could, in the next life, be parented by a couple who would abuse me or by a couple with a dirty old grandfather living with them? Or perhaps become the child of a single mother whose boyfriend would punch me every time I wet my nappy?

If judgement (or *karma*) is something which is weighed and measured meticulously and without mitigation at the end of life on earth, then I will not deserve or be given any kind of promotion in the next. I cannot possibly have deserved the wonderful parents I had in this life. I cannot possibly have deserved the family life I enjoyed over many years. If *karma* is fair, then I have had it! I was pinning my hopes on a spot of mitigation and being able to say, when asked, that I was the brother of Him who died on the cross, and that if the man at the gate cared to peer closely at my forehead, he would see the remains of a cross that had been put there in water 77 years ago at my baptism. At that time, the vicar pronounced that I was made a child of God, a member of Christ and an inheritor of the Kingdom of Heaven. But now this idea of reincarnation is pulling the rug from under my feet. Time now to repeat the same prayer over and over again: 'Into thy hands, O Lord, I commit my spirit.' I certainly have a vested interest in the Christian idea that 'In my father's house are many dwelling places', and if I am lucky I may be offered a tenancy in one of the little cottages, preferably next door to where my parents live.

So I am prejudiced against reincarnation, and I would go to any lengths to be able to prove to myself, and to others, that it is false. It is such a droll, unimaginative idea and yet, as my friend reminded me, there must be something in it for 75 per cent of the world's population to believe in it.

When I asked my spiritualist friends if they believe in reincarnation, I was told they are divided about it – some do and some do not, Others say, 'Yes, we believe in reincarnation, but we believe there is a choice for the individual.' We can choose whether or not we would like to have another go at being a flesh-covered human back on Earth, or whether we would prefer to take up some kind of different occupation in the Summerland, wearing an etheric body. I think it would be true to say that most Spiritualists do believe there is a choice. One could be reincarnated, but it certainly is not compulsory.

I have found amongst my papers a little leaflet published

by the Greater World Association called *Truth Concerning Reincarnation: A Collection of the Teachings of Zodiac,* which I find interesting.

Zodiac is one of the Spiritualist movement's great teacher guides, and he states emphatically over and over again that reincarnation into this world is wrong. He says, 'Belief in reincarnation is wrong – it is brought about by misunderstanding.' But he does speak of the possibility of a new life on some planet other than earth.

Zodiac first manifested himself in 1921 to a small family in West London, and chose a Miss Winifred Moyes to be his medium. He called himself 'Zodiac', refusing to give his earthly name. Many believe he is the teacher in the temple who asked Jesus which was the greatest commandment. For nearly 30 years he gave his teachings through Miss Moyes, and today many of his sayings are in bound volumes.

I would like to believe in Zodiac because apart from comforting me with his statement that reincarnation is wrong, he says other wise things. He explains a great deal that is a mystery to many religious people. Many theologians have realized that if we postulate physical birth, or life on Earth, as the beginning of life, then we create insoluble problems. The great preacher and writer the Reverend Leslie Weatherhead, who as minister of the City Temple in the 1940s, expresses this problem succinctly:

> If I fail to pass those examinations in life which can only be taken whilst I dwell in the physical body, shall I not have to come back and take them again?

This leaves no doubt that at that stage in his life he believed in reincarnation. Then he adds:

> If every birth in the world is the birth of a new soul, I don't see how progress can ever be consummated. Each has to begin at scratch. Each child is born a selfish little animal, not able in character to begin where the most saintly parent left off – there can never be a perfect world unless gradually those born into it

can take advantage of the lessons learned in earlier lives instead of starting at scratch.

This is something I too find difficult to understand. There are millions of births every year. This means millions of new souls clambering on to the big wheel of life. When the big wheel comes to an abrupt stop at the end of time, many will not have had a full turn, some will not have had a turn at all. Zodiac comes up with the answer. He says:

Before Earth life you had many kinds of body and there are conditions in other worlds that are similar to those on the earth plane, but you are born *of the flesh once only*.

Then he goes on to answer Leslie Weatherhead's question:

Before you had physical birth, and in another kind of body – not a fleshly body – you were able to come into these material conditions and to walk with certain souls undergoing the Earth life. This was of the greatest use to you, and that is why some of you seem to remember things, scenes and events.

I like any kind of evidence that helps me reject the idea of a return into this world. But what Zodiac has to say about life before Earth life reminds me a little bit of the Jehovah's Witnesses. You may have noticed that when the Witness brethen come along to disturb your Sunday afternoon meditation, it is only one of them who does the talking. The other two just stand on one side quietly; listening and learning. I have a feeling that there is a strict rule about this, that no member is given permission to speak on someone's doorstep until he has put in an apprenticeship in the company of a senior. Zodiac similarly suggests that souls about to be born to an Earth life have a chance of preview, and that some of us at least have had the advantage of doing the rounds with an experienced Earth-dweller before being given our fleshly body.

I think perhaps the gist of his teaching is that provided we experience the whole curriculum, it doesn't matter which subject we tackle first, or which lecture theatre we patronize first. One thing only is certain: we only need the one physical body, and we need it only for that short period when we pass through the Earth experience. And again he says:

> Life has been in countless spheres and conditions before physical birth, and it will be, after physical death. You are not given the gift of life or of consciousness just for the physical plane. This is but some short stage, and I must emphasize that the physical stage is not repeated, nor do you have more than one body of flesh.

So what of the three quarters of the world's population, those millions who disregard the teaching of Zodiac, who believe and teach that after physical death we discard our physical body, put on another body of flesh and re-enter the same Earth world as a baby boy or girl? The new Evans-Wentz translation of *The Tibetan Book of the Dead* has thrown a great deal of new light on the Buddhist religion, and on our problem. According to this, when a man becomes old, or sick unto death, it is required that there should be read to him for a period of 49 days the description of the Seven Stages of Transition. Should the sick person lose consciousness, or even die, the readings must continue for this set period on the assumption that even if the body is dead, the soul is still capable of hearing and understanding. One of the great truths recited into the ear of the dying person is that he will be allowed to choose for himself after death whether to reincarnate into another body or not. This last statement seems to me much fairer and much more charitable than the statement made in the Athansian Creed:

> And they that have done good shall go into everlasting life [whether they like it or not] and they that have done evil into everlasting fire [whether they like it or not].

This creed seems to me to have been tailor-made for those gentlemen of the cloth who denigrate Canon Henry Scott

Holland and his poem. There is a great deal of evidence for believing in the Buddhist idea that there is a choice between reincarnating and returning to earth and passing on to another stage in an etheric body.

The whole concept of compulsory reincarnation seems very unfair. Throughout my life on earth, my Creator allowed me a freedom of choice (very often to my own cost). It seems irrational that once I am dead, and after only a few decades of this life of free choice, the same Creator should snatch this freedom away from me and give me orders like 'Go to sleep', 'Rest eternal, until I blow the trumpet to tell you your fate at the end of time', or 'Reincarnate and return to earth.'

So as long as the three-quarters of the world's population who believe we come back to this earth in another body agree that there is a choice, I can feel much happier sitting here behind the vicarage sofa.

So the world's religions are somewhat divided about reincarnation. Some seem to say: 'Don't worry about it. See how you feel when the time comes. Nobody's going to push you.' A number reject the idea completely in favour of compulsory eternal rest. And others, including some parapsychologists and the hypnotherapists, seem determined to prove that life goes on and on, on the earth's treadmill. They say they can prove without the shadow of a doubt, that after dying many people return to live another life on Earth, and some of them can even remember incidents from their previous life or lives.

Perhaps the best-known recorded example of such an occurrence is that of Shanti Devi. Shanti was born in 1926 to middle-class parents in Delhi. When she was three, she told her parents that she had been married to a man in another life and that she had had children. Her parents put it down to childish fantasy and gave her stories scant attention. But as she grew older she persisted in her account and gave more detail. Her husband's name, she told them, was Kedarnath and they had lived in a little village called Muttra, not far from Delhi. It was there, she said, that she had died in 1925, while giving birth to their fourth child. At the age of 7, Shanti was quite convinced that she had lived a previous life, and she could remember a great deal about it. Her name, she told them, had been Ludgi.

A business colleague of her father's, a native of Muttra, called at their home one day. Shanti opened the door to him and remembered him immediately. When questioned by her parents, the man said that he had a cousin called Kedarnath and that this cousin had had a wife called Ludgi who had died in childbirth. Without telling Shanti, her parents arranged a test. Before long another stranger called at their door. Shanti recognized him immediately – he was Kedarnath, the husband from her previous life.

The Indian Government then set up an investigation. Shanti was taken to Muttra and there behaved just as if she had never been away from the village. She remembered the names of her in-laws and her neighbours, and when Kedarnath's children were brought forward, she recognized three of them and there were very emotional scenes. She failed to recognize the fourth child, and that was the one who had been born when Ludgi died. As final proof, she told the investigators that Ludgi had buried some rings before she died, and she took them to see the place. They were all convinced that Shanti had lived a previous life in Muttra before being born to her parents in Delhi.

These incidents were reported to an eminent American psychologist, Professor Ian Stevenson, and he came to the same conclusion: that Shanti was a genuine example of reincarnation.

So I surrender. How can anyone argue against such compelling evidence? And yet . . . I hope no one will accuse me of pique or prejudice when I say that I have read many books supporting the idea of reincarnation, and that nearly every author has felt obliged to include the oft-repeated story of

Shanti Devi and one or two other similar stories. And it seems too that it is always the same eminent psychologist, Professor Ian Stevenson, who is given the task of investigating these occurrences.

Possibly the most irrefutable argument for reincarnation is found in the lives and rebirths of successive Dalai Lamas. Even during the life of the reigning Dalai Lama, Tibetan monks begin searching for his successor, or at least the place where his successor might be expected to emerge after his death. And so he goes on living one life on earth after another. And the Buddhists have such a lovely explanation to offer for this. They use the term *bodhisattva* to refer to those beings who, out of compassion for all sentient beings, postpone their own enlightenment so that they can work for the enlightenment of others. Only when the last blade of grass has entered Nirvana does the *bodhisattva* himself enter. If the Dalai Lama could remember all the knowledge he has gathered and all the skills he has mastered, in his many previous lives, he would no doubt be the most enlightened and the most cultured man the world has ever seen.

Psychologists tend to repeat the same half-dozen examples of rebirth, but the examples given by some hypnotherapists are legion. They have concluded that some people have lived more than one life on this earth, and that many can remember a great deal about those earlier lives, and they all use the same method to prove it.

First they set out to find a good hypnotic subject. This is necessary because some people are easy to hypnotize and others are practically impossible. This is why stage and television hypnotists invite about 40 volunteers to the stage before finally rewarding 37 of them with a coloured balloon and sending 37 them back to their seats, retaining just three to assist in the act. Once the subject is in a trance (trance and hypnotism are very similar – the difference is that a trance is self-induced), the command is given for him to begin to regress, or move back in memory over a period of months or years. The hypnotist can allow the regression to carry on at a normal pace, or he can command the subject to regress to a certain period in his life. The hypnotist can also decide to stay at one particular stage of life and examine it in some detail.

Regression has therapeutic uses. A psychiatrist or clinical psychologist may wish to explore in a patient's life one particular incident that has been buried deep in his unconscious mind. He will command the patient to regress year by year until they arrive at that painful incident. The patient will then be asked to describe the awful thing that has been festering in his unconscious mind, and by describing it, will release it and heal the damage it has caused over years. I remember a psychiatrist teacher telling me how he regressed a depressive patient. They travelled backwards through his life stopping at one incident that had caused grief and then at another and arriving eventually at the man's infancy without coming across the real incident that was causing the depression. Then suddenly the patient said: 'Mind my bloody head! You're squashing my bloody head!', and the secret was out. The patient had been a large baby, and his mother had had a small pelvis. The baby had suffered the most excruciating pain in that dark birth passage and it had gone on for a long time. It could only have been his mother who had caused that awful pain. Yet his mother was a blameless, pure, perfect person; she was his whole world, his goddess. If this wonderful person had caused him pain, then he must have deserved it – he must have been a bad, unworthy person. This feeling of badness and unworthiness had been buried deep down in the depth of his mind so that no one would ever know about it. For 50 years, according to the psychiatrist, it had lain festering. Now exposed, the process of cleansing and cauterizing could begin.

But hypnotherapists can also use regression to probe a person's unconscious mind for a different purpose. No one knows who did it first, but somewhere around the 1950s, some of them broke through the memory barrier. Patients had been telling them of incidents from their earliest lives, and describing the painful sensation of birth. Then one patient began recounting tales of another life in another place and at another time.

I have a sneaking feeling that it was an old acquaintance of mine, Arnall Bloxham, who came to live in Cardiff immediately after the war, who first broke the barrier. Bloxham was a wonderful healer. But he was also obsessed with the idea of proving to everyone that reincarnation was a fact, and that they would all return to this world to begin all over again once they were dead.

He used hypnosis as a means of curing physical and psychological illnesses, but he was always on the look-out for any suggestion from any of his patients that would support his belief in reincarnation. Even as a child, Arnall Bloxham believed that he had lived a previous life on this earth and was able to recall incidents from that life. His friends described him as talented artist, but he himself maintained that his art was something carried over from his previous life.

One particular client of Bloxham, a certain Jane Evans, was able at different sessions to recall in great detail seven different lives:

1 As the wife of a Roman officer living in York;
2 As the wife of a rich Jewish merchant living in York in the 12th century;
3 As a servant of the merchant prince Jacques Coeur, living in France in the 15th century;
4 As a Spanish handmaiden in the time of Catherine of Aragon in the early 16th century;
5 As a poor sewing girl in the time of Queen Ann in the early 17th century;
6 As a nun in a convent in Maryland, USA in the early 20th century;
7 As a housewife and secretary in Cardiff in the 20th century.

There are also tapes of a Swansea man, Graham Huxtable,

who must have spent hours on Bloxham's couch describing to him in minute detail his life as a pressed sailor and gunner's mate on board HMS *Aggie* during the Napoleonic Wars. Towards the end of a fierce battle, the poor gunner's mate had his leg shot off. The pain was so great that the patient on the couch was screaming in agony and Bloxham had great difficulty extracting him from his trance.

Jeffery Iverson, who wrote the book *More Lives than One*, describing the work of Bloxham, and also giving the BBC the wonderful programme *The Bloxam Tapes*, tells us that when he met Graham Huxtable whilst researching his book, he found him to have a very soft, pleasant voice. But the gunner's mate's voice he used under hypnosis for Bloxham was much deeper and gruffer and had a south of England country accent. He also used archaic naval slang and spoke of practices aboard ship that were equally antiquated. Yet Huxtable apparently had no connections with, or interest in, the sea. His wartime service had been in tanks, not in ships.

Bloxham used to boast that he had sent a copy of the HMS *Aggie* tape to Lord Mountbatten, who had sent a copy to Prince Philip, and that Prince Philip had had copies made for some of the Admiralty historians because this man who had no knowledge of the sea had explained to his hypnotist how guns were fired in the time of Napoleon, something which until then had remained a mystery to maritime historians.

When Jeffery Iverson first met Bloxham, the hypnotist was an old man, although a very triumphant old man. I am sure that his television programme must have convinced a great number of people that there were for them 'more lives than one'. But the idea that there were to be more lives on this earth must have come as disappointing news for many who had set their hearts on going to Heaven and being with Jesus.

But all is not lost. Some weeks ago a German friend of mine who shares my interest in the paranormal, sent me a cutting of an article written by Melvin Harris in a magazine called *Hypnosis*. There is no date on it and the paper looks a bit faded, so it may have been written some time ago. Mr Harris comes to the conclusion that the apparently impressive Bloxham tapes are proof of cryptomnesia. This means that at some time his patients had read about the characters and the places they talk about on the tapes, and under hypnosis had been able to draw on the knowledge they had gleaned in this way. He then says something that rather surprises me:

> All those who have studied the files of the source material, including Professor Hartley (*and also to his credit Jeffrey Iverson*), now accept that the once impressive tapes are proof of cryptomnesia, and nothing more remarkable than that.

I am quite certain there is no suggestion here that there has been any cheating. From what I have known over the years about Bloxham, I am quite sure he would not have cheated. I have never met Jeffrey Iverson, but I have spoken to him on the phone and I had a long chat with him one Sunday morning, some years ago, on Greater London Radio, with half the population of London listening in to us, and I wouldn't think he was a man to be easily taken in. He in turn had asked the famous investigative journalist Magnus Magnusson to help him research the whole Bloxham chain before he produced the *The Bloxham Tapes*. Iverson describes the tapes as 'the most staggering evidence for reincarnation ever recorded', whilst Magnus Magnusson said of them: 'This story must rank as the most intriguing story I have ever covered.'

So I refuse to allow Mr Harris, in a four-page magazine article, to turn Bloxham's life work into a house of cards, and Jeffrey Iverson's and Magnus Magnussons's researches into Pecksniffian drivel.

The lady crouching with me behind the vicarage sofa is nudging me. She is trying to tell me that Mr Harris is on my side. She is telling me he is destroying very effectively what at first sight appears to be an irrefutable argument for the reincarnation theory that I find so illogical. She is trying to tell me that Mr Harris is my helper. But I say to her: 'Dear madam, I don't need Mr Harris's help to discredit Bloxham's argument because, for all his fine research, he came to a very bad conclusion at the end.'

Arnall Bloxham was a very able researcher and clinician. His tapes are proof of this. He never attempted to lead his patients, and his interviews were entirely unbiased. If this had not been the case, I am quite sure that Jeffrey Iverson and Magnus Magnusson would not have given him the time of day.

But Arnall Bloxham was a convinced reincarnationist. Even as a child he believed fervently that he had lived a previous life, or lives, on this earth. The paintings that decorated the walls of his rambling old house were all of his own making. Some of his friends said that he would probably have made a better living for himself as an artist than he did as a healer. He always insisted that his gift of painting was one he had learned in a previous life and carried over to the present. He believed that many people are able to recall knowledge and craftsmanship learned in one life, and use it to good effect in the next.

Mozart toured Vienna, the Rhineland, Holland, Paris, London and Italy as a concert pianist when he was six years of age, and had already started to compose. At the age of 10, he was appointed master of the Archbishop of Salzburg's Court Orchestra. Mendelssohn composed and performed with his own orchestra as a child. Lord Macaulay, the historian and essayist, had a compendium of his work published before he was eight years old. Bloxham would say of them all that they were able to remember and use in this present life disciplines which they had learned in a previous life.

In the 1950s, one client after another managed to regress past their birth and into what they believed was a previous life. Jeffrey Iverson tells us that when he first interviewed Bloxham, he had to wade through over 400 tapes which produced as evidence of clients' past lives. When the programme *The Bloxham Tapes* appeared and Iverson's book *More Lives than One* flooded libraries and bookshops, this champion of reincarnation must have thrown every hat he possessed into the air. For him it was mission accomplished.

I wrote to Bloxham at the time of his great triumph and suggested that he pick up his hats again. I told him that although I had enjoyed the film and admired his research technique, I was appalled at the way he had drawn his conclusion – it was wrong, illogical and unscientific. He was saying that because Jane Evans, Graham Huxtable and others had described in detail lives lived at the other times and in other places, they themselves must have lived these other lives. I was amazed that a man who had spent most of his life researching the paranormal could have come to such a conclusion. Any practising Spiritualist or student of the paranormal would have been able to tell him that there was nothing very remarkable about the testimonies of Jane Evans and Huxtable; they would be everyday phenomena for them.

I have already mentioned Earth-bound spirits. One night, many years ago, when I took my first steps into the paranormal world, we discovered such a spirit, the ghost of an old publican who had been landlord of a tavern in Denbigh. Two ladies in their early 60s who lived in the house told us how from time to time they and their friends had seen the figure of an old man coming up the cellar steps, crossing the hall, entering the sitting room and then disappearing through the far wall. The ladies found the ghost to be quite innocuous, but their family and friends were rather put off.

A friend of mine, a BBC producer in Bangor, was at this time looking for a good paranormal programme, and paid for the two best mediums in the country at that time to investigate. They did some light probing for information, and said they could see the man who was upsetting the household guests. His name was Eban Jenkins and he had been 90 years of age when he died and had been dead for 30 years, only he didn't know it. In other words, he had become Earth-bound. The mediums' first concern was to release him. This was the first time I had experienced this Earth-bound phenomenon. When he had died Eban Jenkins had failed to find the crossing-over place to enter the Afterlife. Having looked around for some time, he had returned to his old home and continued to live his life as a publican for 30 years. He still came up from the cellar whenever he heard fresh footsteps in the room behind the sitting room that had been his customer bar.

When I told this story in my book *The Holy Ghostbuster*, I had many letters, mostly from elderly people, fearful that this kind of Earth-binding could happen to them. So I must say at this point that earth-bound spirits are very rare, because the rescue squads from the other side are always seeking and offering help to those who wish to cross, and because mediums and sensitives from this side are working with them. I have come to the conclusion that hardly anyone in this world dies a lonely death. The family members that have gone before seem to know when our time has come, and are there with us in the bedroom or in the crashed car, when it comes about. They then take over and lead us across. Amazingly, too, Earth-bound spirits are never worried or unhappy about being Earth-bound because they don't know until they are rescued that they are dead.

To return to Eban Jenkins: one of the BBC's mediums on the night we met him was a short, sturdy, bull-necked man in his late 30s. I have to add that he was a monoglot Englishman. He was sitting in a leather armchair in the middle of the room where we could all see him.

As I have since seen my friend Elwyn Roberts do countless times, he invited Eban Jenkins to use his body. The little man accepted his invitation with alacrity. The room had normal lighting, and in this light I saw the medium change before my eyes. He became paler, his florid face turned death white and became smaller. His whole body became peaked and wizened. I was now looking at an old and very tired man sitting in that huge leather armchair.

We then heard a voice speaking to us from the chair, and it spoke in Welsh: '*Be gythral ma'r holl Saeson ma yn neud yn fy nhy i*? (What the hell are all these English people doing in my house?)' I was the only other Welsh-speaking person in that room, so I was the only one able to converse with the wizened person in the leather chair. I spoke to him for more than ten minutes. When the other medium instructed me to tell him he was dead, the little person become angry and abusive. How dare I say such a thing! He was a man of 90 years and he was still able to manage his tavern single-handed. He spoke in a cracked, squeaky voice, and in pure Denbighshire Welsh.

Strictly speaking all I can say is that I heard the voice, and it came from the region of the leather chair. The person I had seen taking his seat in the chair was a rather large, florid-faced, stockily built gentleman from Birmingham, but the man I was seeing at that moment was no longer thickset and florid; he was pale, fragile and tired-looking. I also knew that the stocky gentleman from Birmingham only knew two words of Welsh – *iechyd da*, whereas the man talking to me spoke fluent old Denbighshire Welsh.

This happened nearly 50 years ago and the mystery was explained to me by the two mediums. The spirit, they said, had accepted the invitation to enter the body of the medium, whose flesh body then acted as a casing for a different etheric body, and that was why we had seen the change. After entering the body, the spirit had instantly made use of its faculties. He had found a perfectly good set of vocal chords and used them to speak in his own native language.

This was my first experience of this kind of phenomenon. Since that day I have come across it many times. I remember once being present at a seance, where Bob Price was the leader. He had just started his philosophy, or what we in church would call the sermon. Suddenly his voice cracked and became piercing and high pitched: 'I am Tim Lem and I come to tell you many things,' he said. 'I will teach you how to hear that silence that has its own music.' He spoke like this for about 20 minutes. Other members told us we have been extremely fortunate to have been able to listen to Tim Lem, a Tibetan monk who had been dead almost 3,000 years and had presumably continued his education and meditations throughout this period. I didn't like to say so, but I didn't think much of his philosophy. I found Bob Price's philosophy which Tim Lem had so rudely interrupted, far more interesting!

I have also heard my friend Elwyn Roberts say to lost or shy ghosts on countless occasions: 'Don't be afraid. Join us. Use my body, if you know how to.' And I must say that most of them accept his invitation with the same readiness with which old Eban Jenkins accepted the invitation of the medium from Birmingham and Tim Lem so rudely did with Bob Price, even without an invitation.

Now the point I wish to emphasize is this. The Birmingham medium would never have dreamed of boasting in his local that he had been a publican in Wales in another life. He could have said, 'Do you know, chaps, on one occasion when I was in deep trance, the ghost of a Welsh publican entered into me and spoke through me in Welsh.' But I do not think he would bother somehow. And it would never have occurred to Bob Price to say to anyone that he had been a Tibetan monk in another life, nor would Elwyn claim that in other lives he had been a Russian forestry worker, a captain in the Indian Army, a cook in the Bron Eifion Hotel in Criccieth, and an arms-bearer for Prince Llewellyn. The mediums and sensitives I know are well aware of what is happening to them when they are in trance or hypnotized. Many of them are able to expel their own ego from its body casing, and for a time entertain within that casing someone else's etheric body or spirit. But then again do they all first expel their own egos? Do they encourage their own egos to enjoy a little out-of-body experience while they accommodate a spirit guest? I have a feeling that some of them just move their own ego a little to one side to allow sufficient room for the guest spirit to lie next to it.

Jeff Iverson makes much of the fact that Jane Evans spoke in different voices. He also tells us that soft-voiced Graham Huxtable spoke in a south of England dialect, but with a very gruff voice, when he became the gunner's mate aboard the HMS *Aggie*. Of course they did. That was the way the different spirits that entered Jane Evans's body did speak and that was the way one would have expected the ghost of the gunner's mate, who for a short time occupied Graham Huxtable's body, to speak. For people who know about the paranormal, there is nothing at all unusual in this. It is just a phenomenon. It doesn't matter anyway, because I never received a reply from Bloxham.

In the letter I wrote to Arnall Bloxham I also told him about my friend Winnie Marshall. I told him that she, like him, had decorated the walls of her house with works of her own creation. But unlike him, Winnie made no claim to having acquired her artistic skills in some prior life. As a matter of fact she had confided to me that left to her own devices she could not draw a picture of an egg. When she fancies a fresh landscape for her dining room, or an anniversary gift for a friend, she takes out her painting gear, holds the brush in her hand and her guides do the rest. She is absolutely certain that her artistic prowess has nothing whatsoever to do with any previous life. I seem to remember too that there was a lady somewhere who had never had a day's piano lesson in her life, yet all she had to do was place her fingers on the keyboard and Mozart and Chopin did the rest.

10   *The Experts*

For me, 1990 was a wonderful year. A London television company invited me to take part in a programme about the paranormal. I was asked to do some scripting and also take part myself. The filming was to take place in Cardiff Castle over three days.

The day I was due in Cardiff there was a rail strike, so the company sent a taxi from Cardiff to Llandegai to get me there by 2 pm. The taxi they sent must have been the biggest limousine the village had ever seen. The driver opened the backdoor. I threw my case in, waved goodbye to my wife, stepped inside and sat where I thought the back seat should have been – and fell flat on the floor. It was 8 am, so fortunately there was no one about to witness my ignominy!

The driver told me that this taxi was well known in Cardiff. It was called 'Archie' because it had at one time belonged to Archbishop Runcie of Canterbury. The Archbishop had had the body extended to give him more working space in the back. I worked out that my bottom must have hit the spot where his desk used to be. But Archie delivered me in Cardiff in good time for lunch, before meeting the others in the castle at 2 pm.

I shall never forget how thrilled and awed I was, walking into the main hall of the castle that afternoon. It was just like

entering Paradise or the Summerland. The first person I saw
was Sian Phillips, that queen of stage and screen. That was
not all; she came up to me; she recognized me; she
remembered my name. She recalled that in the 1960s, when
she was a very young member of the BBC Rep in Cardiff, I
was eking out my parson's pay by working in the BBC Rep
in Bangor. We had often worked together on radio plays.
Sian was gracious enough to remember this and wanted to
know how all the others had fared. Toyah Willcox and
Lynsey de Paul were sitting on a rather large sofa chatting,
and I recognized the writers and researchers Peter and Mary
Harrison. There was also a very charming lady I came to
know as Frances Ommaney, a film producer from Canada.
Shelley Von Strunkel, the American parapsychology
consultant, was there, and the young medium Paul Norten
was chatting to a person whom I was later to know as Peter
Ramster, the writer and psychologist from Australia. Also
present, and looking very elegant in full clericals, was a
Congregationalist minister, the Reverend Graham St John
Willey. Everyone was apparently waiting for Sir David Frost
to arrive. This was news to me. It was the first time for me
to be told that David Frost was to front this programme –
one of several set up investigate the paranormal.

The company, at what must have been fantastic cost, had
gathered together people from across the world who
had had psychic experiences, and also the experts to interpret
these experiences. Toyah, Lynsey and Frances were amongst
those who had had strange experiences. Mary Harrison and
Shelley von Strunkel were there as interpreters. Paul Norten
and Peter Ramster were experts in their own fields, and Sian
Phillips was there to charm the viewers with her readings of
three Welsh ghost stories.

When David Frost arrived, he apologized to everyone for
being five minutes late. He went round kissing the ladies and
shaking hands with the men, all of whom he seemed to know.
I stood in the corner. He won't know me, I thought. But he

did. With hand outstretched, he crossed over to where I was standing. 'Aelwyn,' he said – he knew my name. 'Sorry I'm late, the traffic was awful today.' I'm sure that interviewers do their homework meticulously before interviewing the President of the United States or the King of Siam, but the greatest of all interviewers didn't stop there; he had done his homework meticulously even before meeting the Vicar of Llandegai. And he had done it well, because the next thing he said to me was: 'Give me five minutes to change and I'll be with you.' He knew what I did not, that the filming was to start with him interviewing me and that afterwards we were to move to the ballroom for the second scene. So this was why they had sent Archie the taxi all the way from Cardiff to fetch me. I was on first call.

We sat, David Frost and I, facing each other, cameras focused, sound men and electricians at the ready, and on the order 'Take One', David took off his glasses, pointed them at me and said, 'Aelwyn, tell me . . .' And we were off. I had faced cameras many times before and there had always been two and even three or four takes before the director was satisfied. But on this occasion, we chatted away easily, oblivious of the audience of glittering stars surrounding us. When we had finished, the producer said: 'Next scene in the ballroom.' Talking to David Frost is so easy, we managed the whole thing in one take.

After completing my five-minute chat with David, my camera front work was over. There now remained three days of listening to the experts, talking to them and occasionally disagreeing with them because in 40 years I, too, had picked up a thing or two.

Toyah, Lynsey and Frances told us of out-of-body experiences they had had. Lynsey said that when she was four years of age, after her mother had put her to bed, read her a story, and said prayers with her and switched off the light she would quite often fly out of her body and sit above the chest of drawers looking down at her body. When she told her mother how she flew around the bedroom, her mother would humour her and just say: 'Oh that's nice, darling.' While Lynsey was talking I remembered my friend Elwyn telling a similar tale. At about the same age, he would quite often look down at his own body on the bed. But he didn't tell his mother or anyone else about it, because he thought this kind of thing was something everyone did when they couldn't go to sleep on light summer evenings.

Toyah told us of an experience which could have been either an out-of-body or a near-death experience; it is sometimes difficult to differentiate between the two. There is no doubt at all that many people who die, sitting in a car or at the bottom of a swimming pool or, the most favourite position of all, on the surgeon's operating table, manage to come back again either spontaneously or by physical resuscitation and describe what they experienced. This would be described as a near-death experience. There are others whose egos or personalities, while they are very much alive, escape from their bodies for short periods. During these short periods they are able to look down on their own bodies, and the bodies of others in the same room. This is called an out-of-body experience, and many examples have been reported from dental surgeries. Psychologists even suggest that some of us can will ourselves into this experience as an act of retaliation or revenge against the dentist.

We are terrified of him with his drill and his instruments. Then all of a sudden we find we can transport ourselves to the ceiling of his surgery and see him running around in panic, sweating, pummelling the chest of our body in the chair, trying the kiss of life, until we decide to come back to our body. To have a grandstand seat watching a discomfited dentist must be worth his fee any day!

Frances Ommaney gave a most graphic description of a near-death experience. She had got into difficulties whilst bathing. She knew she was drowning, and then found herself looking down at the whole scene. She could see a hand protruding from the sea. On the second finger was a ring which she recognized as one she had worn ever since she was a child. From her new vantage point she felt no fear. The hand was not coming up so regularly now, but she was not a bit worried. She could see the rescue team on the shore preparing to go out to save her and she remembered thinking quite matter of factly, Oh good, I am going to be saved. Whilst this was going on, she decided to go and find her boyfriend, who had been with her in the water. She was in time to see him jumping on to his motor bike and riding away like fury. He hit a kerb, grazed his knee, jumped back on his bike again and was off at speed. After seeing that he was all right, Frances decided to go back to the beach and see how her rescue was going. Her rescuers had her on a stretcher by now. The young one was looking very sad – near to tears, she thought – because he was obviously convinced she was dead.

Then all of a sudden she found herself not looking down on them as before, but looking up at their faces. She smiled at them, and they very nearly dropped the stretcher in their joy. Frances then added: 'And after all that, the rescuers and the hospital people confirmed that there was not a drop of water in my lungs.' I never quite understood why she said that. Someone on the set asked her whatever had possessed her boyfriend to run away and she replied: 'He was a bit of a coward and he was very young. But he was mystified when I told him how I had seen him fall off his bike and graze his knee.'

I think, although I am not entirely sure, that Frances, was telling us about a near-death experience. Lynsey, and possibly Toyah, were talking about out-of-body experiences. OBE is something which very often happens spontaneously. But it can also be cultivated. There are a great many mystics, and non-mystics, who work very hard at the craft of leaving their body and floating above it, and, in time and after more practice, travelling from room to room and eventually from place to place. The Russians are great OBE students. Sylvan

Muldoon and Hereward Carrington wrote a book about it which is now regarded as a classic 'DIY' manual. It warns that it is not by any means an easy thing to accomplish. It takes a lot of practice and dedication. For the persevering, the name of the book is *The Projection of the Astral Body*, and it is published by Rider.

I remember being told the story of the wonderful Italian monk Padre Pio. He was the abbot of a closed monastic order, and never set foot outside his monastery gates. Yet there were a great number of the poor in villages around the monastery prepared to swear that when a child had been ill, or when they were without food the day before Christmas, Padre Pio had visited their home and their child had been cured or they had food aplenty for Christmas.

I learned little that was new to me from Paul Norten, the medium. He explained his mediumship exactly as I had heard Winnie Marshall explaining hers. 'We don't call spirits; they call us.' He talked of his guides and teachers in exactly the same way as Winnie described hers.

Then came the Reverend Graham St John Willey, the Congregationalist minister. David Frost asked him what he made of the young medium's remarks. He replied that he thought the whole process described by Paul Norten, and I thought by implication by the rest of us too, was demoniac. 'He mistakenly thinks', he said, 'that he is communicating with guides and teachers from the other world. But there is not the slightest doubt, that he is communicating with the angels of the devil, the angels that were cast out of Heaven with their master at the beginning of time.'

I felt sorry for the young medium. He seemed quite amazed, and very hurt, at this unexpected attack. David Frost snatched off his glasses and pointed them at the Reverend. 'Tell me, Graham,' he said, 'on what authority do you say this?' And as I had anticipated, Graham replied: 'On the authority of the Word of God.' Then he proceeded, as I knew full well he would, to tell the story of Dives and

Lazarus. He emphasized the bit about Abraham's bosom and seemed somehow to make the gulf between the dead and the living even wider than it was in the Gospel. 'These are the words of Jesus,' he said, but he did not say in what context Jesus had spoken them. It was perfectly obvious that young Paul Norten had never been to Sunday school in his life, or had not been blessed with a very good teacher if he had. He probably knew as much about the Bible as the Reverend Willey knew about the *Collection of the Teachings of Zodiac*. The minister also told us, in no uncertain terms, that Jesus had said it was wrong to communicate with the dead. We were all being put in our places, not just Paul Norten. It was so unfair, the cameras were whirling and I was squirming on the outside of the circle. Each discussion circle had been carefully chosen and I was not part of this one. I was not even dressed suitably to gatecrash it. Paul was the one in the line of fire, but the rest of us had to take cover against the flack. And all the time I knew, from my own knowledge of the same Word of God, that the Jesus whom Graham said had taught that communing with the dead was a sin had done the very same thing Himself. Jesus had enjoyed the experience immensely and He had taken with Him, to the transfiguration seance, three of His disciples. They too had enjoyed the experience immensely. Peter had even wanted to build tents there, so that they could all stay in this place with the spirits of the dead. I was hoping that David Frost – himself a son of the Manse – would say: '"Hold it, Rev." My father always used to say in Sunday school . . .', but he didn't.

Then some guide or teacher, or perhaps Zodiac himself, must have placed a 2-inch nail between the positive and negative terminals of the camera. It sparked violently, there was a smell of burning, and filming had to be discontinued. During this break I was able to rush to Toyah and tell her quickly that Jesus was in actual fact a much cleverer medium or clairvoyant than Paul would ever be and that when He wanted a break, He took three of His disciples with Him to a mountain where they met and talked to the ghosts of Moses and Elijah. So how dare the Reverend Graham St John Willey say that when Paul Norten was conversing with the dead he was doing something that was demoniac and evil?

Toyah is as intelligent as she is pretty. She took in my garbled sermon, and as soon as the camera was repaired and the man had called 'Take Two,' she came out with it. 'But I thought it says in the Bible that Jesus went to a mountain to talk to the ghosts of Moses and Elijah.' She said her piece very well, but when I saw the edited film her little sermon had been cut out.

Frost's Night Visitors was not a good programme. It amazes me to think of the expert knowledge brought together from Britain, American, Canada and Australia, and how little use was made of it. Will Aaron, my favourite producer, given the cast we had, would had produced a programme to remember. But listening to the vast exchange of paranormal knowledge and experimental results that went on in Cardiff Castle over those three days was a tremendous experience.

At first I found myself just listening casually to discussions about reincarnation while pretending not to. I then met Peter Ramster. Peter is a writer and a psychologist from Australia, a person of great charm and knowledge. I had gone to Cardiff as a sworn anti-reincarnationalist. Peter, I found, was a younger version of Arnall Bloxham. Like Bloxham, he had spent his life encouraging patients to regress to previous lives. But unlike Bloxham, he was also a meticulous researcher. He had transported many of his dual-life clients half across the world so that they could visit the places where they said they had lived before, and where he could verify their statements.

He cited the case of a woman patient in Australia, who he knew had never left that country. She described to him in detail the life she had lived in a Yorkshire village 200 years before. Peter brought her to England and went with her to the village. From the minute she stepped out of the car she knew her way about. 'All this is new around here,' she said. But the village cross was there and so was the Stag Inn. She was also overjoyed to find too that her former home was still standing. She had told Peter in Australia that she remembered burying some trinkets at the old house. They dug and the trinkets were found exactly where she said. His patient showed unerring knowledge of the village of 200 years ago and of the people who lived there. Local historians were amazed at her knowledge; church records as well as those at Somerset House registers, where all British births marriages and deaths are recorded, confirmed it.

When I first heard this story, I put it down as another 'Shanti Deva' story and told myself that he would soon be telling the listeners how he invited a very ancient Professor Ian Stevenson to investigate the incident. But Peter who, like Bloxham, had numberless case reports, had no need to call in outside investigators. As a psychologist, he did his own researching and he did it well.

At this point, Mary Harrison asked Peter a question I had never heard asked before: 'Did you apply the hypnosis test to your subjects?' Peter said he hadn't because the factual evidence provided by all his patients, and particularly by the 'Yorkshire' woman, was so convincing that he didn't think it was necessary. Mary insisted that having gone to the trouble, and to the great expense, of transporting both himself and his patient from Australia to Yorkshire, it was a pity he had not spent five minutes conducting the hypnosis test. It was at this point that I moved a little closer to the reincarnation circle. Mary explained that if anyone claimed to have been the Mary Queen of Scots in a different life, or even to have been plain Joe Bloggs, all that was necessary to verify the claim was to re-hypnotize them and to ask them 'When did you first hear the name Mary Queen of Scots?', or 'When did you first hear about Joe Bloggs?' The hypnotized person would always give a truthful answer – 'I read about her in a book when I was ten,' or 'My grandmother used to tell us stories about Joe Bloggs.'

Strangely enough, I no longer felt as afraid of the idea of reincarnation as I had before. I was prepared to talk about it, and I knew the man to talk to was Peter Ramster. He was a very gentle and a very persuasive man. If anyone had told me that his ancestors had lived in Ireland and that before moving to Australia 200 years ago had had long sessions kissing the Blarney Stone, I would have believed him. 'My dear Aelwyn,' he said when he saw me beginning to get ruffled, 'I believe exactly as you do about reincarnation. Of course, this earth existence of ours is our beginning, our Standard One, and of course you are right when you say that after Standard One, we normally move on to Standard Two. But, can't you imagine, on some rare occasion, the Headmaster coming to Standard One during the last week of the school year and telling the children, 'When you come back after the holidays you will all be moving to Standard Two, all of you, that is, except William here. You all know that William had an accident this year, and he has been very brave. But it has meant that he has had to miss school for many months. Now we think it would be better for William to stay another year in Standard One, so that he can catch up before moving to Standard Two.'

And then, smiling at me, he proceeded to say: 'As a minister of religion, Aelwyn, I am sure you will have told your parishioners about the importance of living a full and fruitful Earth life, making progress in this life before moving to the next.' I was nodding agreement to all this, but when this apostle of reincarnation had baited the trap, he pulled the spring. 'So,' he said, 'What of the thousands of little children who are aborted, or stillborn, or killed in accidents? None of these were given the chance to experience this Earth life that you, as a minister, say is so important.' I wanted to tell him that my Spiritualist friend had told me that the nurseries and schools in the Summerland were coping with this problem. But then I thought if this is the case, and the Summerland is able to cope, why bother with Earth life at all? So I let him carry on.

'My case book,' he said, 'gives me sufficient evidence for believing that aborted children, and other children who die young, are reborn again to other parents; baby boys sometimes reborn as baby girls and vice versa. And on rare occasions, I have come across evidence of a child dying and then being reborn to his original parents.'

What this man was telling me was making sense, and he was obviously a very meticulous and honest researcher. Mary Harrison agreed with him. She said there were, to her certain knowledge, hundreds of small children up and down the country claiming that they could remember previous lives. They would begin a conversation by saying, 'My other mummy and daddy told me . . .' or 'I remember coming here with my other mummy.' Mary read us a letter she had received that day from a mother.

I took my three-year-old boy Tom with me to Derby some months ago. As far as I can recollect it was my first visit ever to Derby – it was most certainly Thomas's first visit. As soon as we got to the town centre, Tom asked me where the tower was. He told me that when he was here last with his other mummy, there was a tower in the middle of the shops, and he wanted to go and see it. I tried to put him off by telling him it was a dream. But he still went on about his precious tower. Recently I read in a newspaper how workmen, demolishing buildings in Derby town centre, had come across the foundations of an old tower.

Mary was asked if this could be regarded as proof of reincarnation. Her reply was yes and no: 'yes' because Tom might be quite correct when he said he had seen a tower in the centre of Derby in a previous life, and 'no' because it could be that Tom had never been to Derby in this or any other life, but that he knew about the tower because, at his conception he had inherited some of his great great grandmother's genetic memory. In the same way as we inherit genes for our parents' and ancestors' physical characteristics, so we can also receive some of our ancestors' memories. Mary said that before she could make up her mind one way or the other, she would need to know how much knowledge of Derby Tom's great great grandparents had had.

There are many such cases to be found around the country. Normally the children are usually precocious, and they begin to talk about their previous lives when they are two or three years of age. Their stories usually embarrass their parents, who tend to deal with them either by ignoring them or by scoffing at them. Most are successful, and by the time the children are six or seven they have forgotten all about it.

This was strong stuff for die-hard anti-reincarnationalist. However I slept on it and in the morning, like the curate with his egg, I decided that I liked parts of it. I found it easier to accept this theory about aborted and stillborn children than the one propounded by a certain Dr McAll, who worked as a consultant psychiatrist in Manchester in the 1960s and 1970s. He realized that he had been treating a dispro-portionate number of women patients in the 20 to 30 age group who suffered from depression and other psychiatric disturbances such as schizophrenia. He dealt with 200 such patients in a period of 18 months, and discovered that there was a common denominator in their complaint: a majority had had either an abortion or a miscarriage during the previous seven years. He therefore suggested that they, and their families, were being haunted by the ghosts of their aborted or miscarried children.

He requested the services of 70 clergymen in the diocese of Manchester and asked them to conduct a unique form of exorcism. He asked them to conduct funerals, without bodies, for the dead babies. These funerals were conducted within the framework of the communion service. They were attended by the families, the babies were given names and their souls committed to God. The clergy and members of the families attending these services testified to having seen amazing things happen – in most cases there had been dramatic improvements in the patients' health.

Dr McCall discovered that it was not just the mother's of aborted children that were being troubled by them. Other members of the family suffered too. He reports how he was treating a young girl of 17 who was depressed and had strong suicidal tendencies. During treatment he discovered that this patient's mother had had an abortion before her marriage and had kept it a secret from her family.

The doctor arranged the usual funeral service for this long-aborted child and attended himself as was his custom. He said that during the service he saw Jesus descending from the wooden cross on the altar and going up to the mother and embracing her. The mother also testified: 'I saw Jesus at that service. He told me my baby's name was June – so she must have been a girl.'

After the service the mother went home to her mentally ill daughter and told her all about it and how she had been told by Jesus that her first daughter's name was June. Her sick daughter replied: 'Oh mummy why didn't you tell me this. She had been coming to me for a long long time and telling me she is my big sister and asking me to help her. I wish you had told me. From that very day the depression and the suicidal tendency left the young girl. That same year she was able to sit her A Levels and enter University.

A Manchester social worker told how his depressed wife became a patient of Dr McAll. The doctor discovered that she had had an abortion seven years earlier. The social worker reported:

> The next day, early in the morning, a shadowy figure appeared at our bedside. My wife said, 'If you are my little boy welcome to the family.' The figure sat down on the bed and my wife dissolved in tears. Next day we had a church service for the child. Since then there has been a marvellous change in my wife, and our house, which we believe was haunted, is now at peace.

I have no doubt that Dr McAll and his army of clergymen restored joy and peace to many homes in and around Manchester, but my whole being rebels against the idea, or the dogma, that lies behind these cures. It requires that we believe there are dead children who should be in Paradise or the Summerland, or whatever our faith teaches us to call the next life, but who have not entered this second stage. They are still here on Earth, dressed in their spirit bodies, and their spirit bodies are growing at the same rate as Earth bodies grow. The baby, aborted 20 years before, looked about 20 years of age when her sister saw her. When the boy, aborted seven years before, sat on his mother's bed, he appeared to be about seven years of age. Were they Earth-bound until Dr McAll and his team rescued them?

The teenage girl told her mother that her aborted sister had come to her to ask for help. But this is not a discovery peculiar to Dr McAll. I too have come across aborted and stillborn children living under the same roof as their mother. The ones I have met have been very happy living this in-between life, but are they Earth-bound? It is their ageing at the same rate as humans that worries me and makes me fear that they are. I know one boy spirit of 13 with curly blond hair and blue, blue eyes. People who saw him 40 years ago described him as being 13 years of age, and said he had a ball in his hand which he would throw against the kitchen wall. People who saw him last week told me he still looks 13 and he still brings his ball with him and throws it against the kitchen wall. I regard this as healthy behaviour – in a spirit. This boy is not Earth-bound; he is coming down to have a look at us from time to time, and so that he can be recognized when he does revisit earth he dresses in his old Earth clothes.

Many spirits, for good measure are prepared to wear their old Earth watches and chains across their fat waistcoated stomachs. But I am not sure about Dr McAll's babies. If he is right, how many thousands of other little unwanted children are there, growing up amongst us, haunting us and casting a mantle of depression and sadness over the homes of families who rejected them?

I have re-read Peter Ramster's book *The Search for Lives Past* and I find it most comforting. I do hope he is right and that small children who die are given a second chance of experiencing this funny Earth life of ours.

Of all the wonderful things that happened to me during my three days at Cardiff Castle I have but one regret. I do wish I could I have met Mary Harrison and learned about the hypnosis test before Arnall Bloxham died. It would have been very interesting to know what reply Jane Evans would have given when asked when she had first heard of Rebecca the Jewess, who lived in York in the 12th century, and how Graham Huxtable first came to know about the HMS *Aggie*.

11   *The Benefit Match or Plot 7*

—

In the football world, when a player retires after serving the same club for 10–15 years, his colleagues often arrange a benefit match for him. They tell me the gate money from a benefit match between two first-division teams could amount to thousands of pounds.

I have been working with ghosts for over 40 years and I have never received a brass farthing for my efforts. Very often Elwyn and I have had to pay our own out-of-pocket expenses. During these years we have helped release a few people who were Earth-bound, and have counselled a good number of spirits who were finding it difficult to settle down on the other side because they had unresolved problems on this side. We have acted as social workers amongst the spirit fraternity for a good many years. But there has been no mention of a benefit match, or even a 'Thank you very much.'

Or that was what I thought until quite recently. During the last few months, however, I have come to realize that my spirit friends, bless them, did arrange a benefit match for Elwyn and me in their own way. But it took me five years to realize what they had done. It was not a money benefit match because these people don't deal in money. What they did give me was a story plot, and I have a feeling that it is a 'Plot 7'.

There is a saying amongst fiction writers that there are

only six different story plots in existence. All the stories, novels, plays and television dramas are just variations on these six plots. It is also said that if any writer could discover a seventh plot, he could become a Jeffrey Archer or a Catherine Cookson overnight.

I don't think I have ever read a ghost story in my life. I have seen ghost-story books on my children's bookshelves, big hefty volumes, and I would imagine that their writers, like the writers of all other fiction, are confined to the six-plot rule. But I think my spirit friends have tried to give me a 'Plot 7' story of their own devising, and I am so very much afraid of not being good enough a writer to do it justice. But I have to try.

It was September, five years ago that Mrs Gillian Eames called to see me at the vicarage. She was a pleasant, young-looking, middle-aged lady. She had lived the greater part of her married life on a council estate in Bangor. She had four daughters, two of them married and living away from home and another recently married and living at home until she and her husband could find a place of their own. The youngest was 19, single and fancy-free and also lived at home.

I was not sure why Mrs Eames had called to see me. She most certainly had a ghost in her house – there was not much doubt about that. But on the other hand, neither she nor her family were afraid of ghosts. They were all used to them. She and her husband couldn't remember a time when they were without a family ghost sharing their hearth. They had a ghost, she told me, when the children were small, and when they moved to a bigger house the ghost moved with them. Ever since the girls were little they had been brought up with the idea that there was a spirit living in the house, and imagined every family had a ghost and didn't even mention it to their school friends. The ghost was regarded almost as part of the family They had come to the conclusion that it was a female spirit, and they treated it as a bit of a joke. If a door banged upstairs, if there was a creaky noise in the bedroom, if part of the house became cold all of a sudden, or if there was a strong smell of lavender water in the bathroom, when none of them used lavender water, they would blame the ghost and say: 'She's been at it again.' If one of the girls was certain she had left her watch on the breakfast table but could not find it, she would be told. 'She's probably put it away somewhere safe for you.'

The spirit lodger was also apparently very house-proud, and liked to see things put away in neat little piles. Mrs Eames told me that she had mentioned the ghost to neighbours, and they had jokingly said that if the ghost was house-proud, it would have to be the ghost of old Elizabeth Pritchard, who had lived in the house before them. She apparently spent all her time cleaning and polishing and dusting. Her poor husband had to take his shoes off at the front door and wear carpet slippers in the house.

After hearing Mrs Eames's story, I wondered again why she had bothered to come to see me. She had a ghost most certainly, but it didn't seem to worry anyone. I said so, and she readily agreed. No, she certainly didn't want Elwyn and me to call because she realized we had far more urgent cases to attend to. As a matter of fact, she was quite apologetic about coming. She appeared embarrassed and having told her tale, she seemed like a child who had completed an errand and wanted to return home as soon as possible.

With the hindsight of five years, I have come to believe she was sent to the vicarage; I think her guide escorted her here. But six months later she was back. Things had changed; the ghost had become more obstreperous. Since seeing me, Mrs Eames had been to see her parish priest. He had celebrated communion in the house with the family, but things were no different. The curate had called and he had said a special prayer in every room in the house, but if anything, things were worse.

'Nothing that you can put your finger on,' she said. 'The same noises, only louder and more often. We all think it's because of the baby,' she added.

Heather, the married daughter, who was living at home, was now six months pregnant. Almost as soon as she discovered she was having a baby, she had gone out and bought a rush cot. From the first night she had installed the cot in the bedroom, she had heard creaking noises in the middle of the night. She had also started buying little matinée coats and socks, and had wrapped them in tissue paper and placed them in the top drawer of the chest of drawers. In the night both she and her husband had heard creaking noises coming from the cot, and also the sound of the top drawer being opened and the soft rustle of tissue paper as if the little parcels were being examined. But the moment the light was switched on the rustling stopped.

Mr Eames told me they were all becoming worried at the new goings-on in the house – worried more about the baby than anything else. I assured her that I had never heard of a ghost doing physical harm to a human, and that even poltergeists, which throw and break things, seem to aim to miss a human target. But I told her I would have a chat with Elwyn and that we would probably arrange to call.

We did call a few days later. It was the afternoon of a very hot summer's day and we called in passing. Mrs Eames was home, but the girls were at work. We walked from room to room and Elwyn, even on this hot afternoon, could sense that the house was tenanted by a spirit. He even found the place which she regarded as her own little niche. And he was able to tell us too that on that particular afternoon the ghost was out. The idea of the ghost being being away from home rather amused me, and I had an urge to say: 'Gone shopping to Safeway's perhaps, but I refrained.

Elwyn looked out of the front bedroom window and asked Mrs Eames if she knew the name of the farm down below. Then, Mrs Eames and I both looked out of the window, but neither of us could see a farmhouse of any description. All we could see were rows of terraced council houses, each one with its own pocket-sized front garden and green metal gate. But Elwyn described the scene below as a white-washed smallholding with its own outbuildings. He even described the two dogs and the tractor lying idle in the tidy yard. Then he said: 'There is a name comes to mind. I think that little farmhouse is called Bryn Llwyd Isaf and I have a feeling there is a connection between it and your ghost visitor.' I never argue with Elwyn about what he can see, because I never know which pair of eyes he is using at any given time.

We went downstairs, had a cup of tea, and promised to come another day when the rest of the family were home. But in spite of our promise it was some time after the baby was born that we were able to meet the whole family under the same roof. The baby had weighed 6 lb 5 oz when born, and from the first night she had been brought from hospital and placed to sleep in the cot, it had creaked in the middle of the night. As the baby's mother said, there was no way a 6 lb 5 oz baby could make a cot creak, not even a rush cot. She was also convinced that the little matinée coats in the chest of drawers were being rearranged and refolded.

We had hardly had time to sit in the front parlour before Elwyn announced that we were being joined by a lady visitor. 'She is a young woman and she is dressed in a long cape with a hood attached – a nurse perhaps,' he said. 'On the other hand,' he added, ' the dress is cream rather than the white one would expect of a nurse, and the texture is thicker, more like wool than the cotton of a nurse's uniform. She looks more like a nun than a nurse and she keeps repeating the figure 34 to me.'

It was now time for me, the interrogator, with my clipboard on my knee and my pen in my hand, to start a dialogue. 'Why do you say 34, my dear?' I said 'Is that your age, or do you mean the year 1934 as the year you were born? Or is it the year when you died perhaps?'

'She says 1934 is the year when she died,' Elwyn said. And

then he corrected himself. 'No, she tells me the year 1934 is the year when she committed suicide. She is brimming over wanting to talk to us. Her name is Catherine Anne Hughes and she is a trainee nurse. And,' he added, 'She wants me to tell you, Aelwyn, that she is Anne with an "e".'

So I tried again, 'Catherine Anne with an "e",' I said, 'you are being most helpful. Will you give us the exact date of your death in 1934?'

'It was 15 June; early in the morning,' came the prompt rely, and then followed the story, unfolded in the minutest detail. Her home was in the village of Llanberis, 10 miles away. She had come to the County Hospital, Bangor, a building some 400 yards from where we were sitting, to train to be a nurse. It was her ambition to become a missionary, like her brother. But she had fallen in love with a student called Arthur and had become pregnant. She had not told Arthur, and she knew she would never be able to tell her parents because such a scandal would kill them. Her father, she told us, was an official at Llanberis Slate Quarry, and he was also an elder of the church there.

I know from past experience how ghosts can waffle on and on without giving any information that can be checked. So I decided that Catherine Anne would have to be asked for checkable facts. I broke in or her garrulousness. 'What was your father's name?' I asked.

'Robert Godfrey Hughes, and my mother was Catherine Eluned Hughes,' came the prompt reply.

'Where in Llanberis did you live?'

'In a large detached house with a high wall of slate slabs around it, called Wenfro.'

I asked her to repeat the name of the house. 'Wenfro' didn't seem quite right to my mutation-tuned Welsh ears. I would have expected the article *y* to have preceded the word 'Wenfro' – 'Y Wenfro' – the word to be or alternatively 'Gwenfro'. But Catherine Anne confirmed that the name was Wenfro, as though to say 'Let's get on with it, old man. Let's not waste time splitting hairs.'

It appeared that after finding she was pregnant she decided to take her own life rather than shame her family. Early on the morning of 15 June 1934 she walked out of the County Hospital, came along the little path and up towards the stream, and it was here that she had 'done' it.

'How?' I asked.

'I cut my wrists with a scalpel from the hospital.'

She went on to tell us that the farmer from the nearby farm had found her lying bleeding in his field. He had carried her to the farm, and it was here in the farm that she had died before help could be summoned from the hospital. She then went on to tell us the name of the farm – Bryn Llwyd Isaf. This was the farm Elwyn had seen through the window months before and he had told us then that Bryn Llwyd Isaf could have some connection with the Eameses' ghost. She went on to tell us about the couple who lived on the farm. Griffith and Elin Thomas. Griffith, she told us, had joined the spirit world in 1939 and Elin had died, aged 72, in 1940. Everything was carefully spelt out. Many details were painstakingly repeated for the sake of clarity. Dates, times and place names were carefully emphasized. Somebody was making quite sure I was getting it all down correctly.

I asked more checkable questions. 'Where were you buried?'

'Llanberis,' she said.

'Where in Llanberis? Which church, St Padarn or St Peris?'

There was a pause at this point. Then slowly and deliberately came the reply: 'I was buried in the Red Chapel.' Then she repeated it it in Welsh: '*Mi ges i fy ngladdu yn Capel Coch*'. I had known all the time she was Welsh speaking and that she would have preferred to carry on the conversation in Welsh. But we also knew that the Eameses were English-speaking and after all, the interview was more for their benefit than for ours.

Most of the nonconformist chapels in Wales are named

after the biblical towns of the Old Testament – Bethlehem, Moriah, Beulah, Jerusalem. So I thought that one in a small village like Llanberis which was called the Red Chapel would not be too difficult to find.

I was quite prepared to pass on to fresh pasture at this point, but Catherine Anne was not. She was leaving nothing to chance. 'The Red Chapel,' she said, 'has three doors set in its frontage, and there are steps leading up from the driveway up to the three entrance doors. Above each porch there is a tall arched window with pillars between each window. Stand in the driveway,' she continued, 'and then walk up the stone steps to the centre door. When you are by the centre door, turn your head to the left and there at the far lefthand corner of the chapel you will see my grave. It is marked by a small white marble cross.' Nothing could be clearer.

Never had Elwyn and I come across a spirit from the beyond willing to give such detailed information about a previous life on earth. There were even little irrelevancies thrown in, like the fact that the old school was a cemented building and had a particularly high gable wall, and that the teacher's name was Huw Thomas and he had wavy hair and a big moustache. Elwyn also told us he had a feeling that throughout Catherine Anne's narration, there was a man standing next to her. He was convinced this man was farmer Griffith Thomas, the man who had found her bleeding in his field and in whose house she had died.

Our aim that evening was to give the Eames family some kind of idea why this seemingly unrelated ghost had attached herself to them, and was showing such interest in their baby. We encouraged them to put their own questions to the nurse. Rachel, who had lost her own baby four years earlier, had already told us that in the past the spirit activity had centred around her rather than the other girls. But now it seemed as if Heather, the new mother, was the favoured one. It was Rachel who asked the first question: 'Did you feel sorry for me when I lost my first little baby?' she asked.

And before Catherine Anne could answer, Heather fired her question: 'Do you love my little baby?'

Elwyn told us the answer to both questions was 'Yes, yes.' Catherine Anne, he told us, was so pleased the girls knew how she felt about them. She wanted them to know that she, like Rachel, had lost her own baby and now they could all love and enjoy Heather's baby. This clinched matters for the Eames family. We felt that Mrs Eames had already accepted a fifth daughter into the family, and the girls were ready to welcome a new sister. Mrs Eames was sobbing unashamedly, and the four girls were making liberal use of the tissue box on the coffee table.

Whilst this was going on, Elwyn told us that Catherine Anne was moving closer to the circle. 'Look to the left of me from where you are sitting,' he said.

Instantly there was a gasp from the women. Elwyn asked them if they could see anything. Almost in chorus they replied: 'We can see her hand. Her hand is resting next to yours on the arm of your chair.'

It was after midnight when Elwyn and I wended our way home. He had left his car outside the vicarage in Llandegai and I was chauffeuring him the 2 miles to pick it up. As I drove, I talked checking and cross-checking on all the things we had been told that evening. I had an uneasy feeling that the Coed Mawr estate had been built before 1934. If that was the case, then the nurse would not have been able to walk out of the County Hospital, along the little path and up the stream as she said she had done.

We were nearly home when I became aware of a blue flashing light behind us. It was a police car and I drew up to the curb. I opened my window and saw a young policeman approaching with some kind of bag in his hand. 'Did you think I was drunk or something, officer?'

'Oh, it's you, Vicar,' said the officer. 'Didn't recognize you – you've changed your car.' Then he rather furtively put whatever he had in his hand behind his back. 'I'll be honest with you, Reverend,' he continued. 'It is after midnight. Your car seems to be be the only one on the road. It's a dead straight road from Bangor to Llandegai, and yet you were doing only 20 miles an hour. You will appreciate, that this kind of carry-on does make us chaps just a little suspicious. Anyway I see you're all right so I'll bid you good morning.' And off he went with whatever he had had behind his back now safely tucked inside his tunic. Elwyn could not disguise his disappointment at not seeing a parson breathalysed within the precinct of his own incumbency.

I couldn't wait to start my checking the next day. I rang up the Town Hall to ask when the Coed Mawr Estate had been built. It was 1942, eight years after the suicide. I then sped along to the Archivist's Office in Caernarfon, and asked for an Ordnance Survey map of the area covering Coed Mawr Estate. The most recent they could offer was a 1918 edition which showed the County Hospital and also a little path leading west into the neighbouring field. Catherine Anne had said, 'I turned a little to the left and I came to the stream.' And there on the map was the stream and not 10 yards from it was the little farm with its outbuildings. The farm was clearly named on the map as Bryn Llwyd Isaf, the name Catherine Anne had mentioned the night before, and the name Elwyn had given to it before we had even met her. Check and double check.

I could hardly contain myself. This was going to be the most interesting, the most factual interview anyone had ever had with a spirit from the Beyond. Even members of the Spiritualist faith had never experienced a happening such as this! Nothing comparable had been recorded by Sir Oliver Lodge, Sir William Crookes, Lord Dowding or Hannen Swaffer. It would now be for me to write an accurate account of all that had happened, and submit it to the Psychical Research Society. There would also have to be articles for *Psychic News* and *Two Worlds* magazine. Everything that had been said the previous night would now have to be recorded. Fortunately there had been witnesses present. What had happened in this council estate house in Bangor, North Wales, was going to have very loud repercussions throughout the psychic world.

I next rang the Registrar of Births, Marriages and Deaths in Bangor. I asked if she could give me the names of all the people who had died in the city on 15 June 1934. She rang me back half an hour later. Bangor has a population of 15,000 and I could hardly believe it when she told me that not a single person – man, woman or child – had died on 15 June 1934.

I was bitterly disappointed, but messages from the Other Side, especially messages about dates and times, can be vague. Spirits are never good at dates. The year could have been 1924, the the date could have been 14 or 16 June. I decided I would go to the registry another time and have a good look through the records myself. In the meantime, Llanberis was the place for me. When I parked my car in the High Street of this little mountain village, the first house name to catch my eye was Wenfro. It was spelt exactly as the nurse had spelt it the previous night. But it didn't have a high wall of slate slabs around it, and it was a terraced house, not the grand detached house that she had described to us. But that was for later. My mission now was to find the Red Chapel.

I stopped the first lady I saw crossing the street and asked her if she could direct me to the Red Chapel – 'Capel Coch' I said to her in Welsh, so that there should be no mistake. I was getting a bit nervous by now and I was half afraid she would shrug her shoulders and tell me she didn't have a clue, but she didn't. 'Go on about 50 yards', she said, 'And you will come to the Spar shop on the corner. Turn left and you will find Capel Coch at the end of the road.' She then added quite cheerfully, 'The road is called Red Chapel Road.' I couldn't get there quickly enough.

I followed her direction and there it was, a massive nonconformist chapel with 'Capel Coch 1777' carved above its three doors. It was exactly as the spirit had described it to us. I didn't want to spoil the anticipation. I wanted to see it just as she had said. So I kept the my head down, walked up the four steps and stood facing the middle door. I then took a deep breath and turned my head to look to the left as she had instructed.

There was nothing – no grave, no white cross to the left or the right. All I could see was a tangle of briars that had been cut weeks before and left to rot. The cross could have been moved, I thought. I hurried down the steps and around to the back of the chapel. There was not a grave anywhere in sight. Red Chapel was a chapel without a cemetery or a churchyard of any kind.

Later I discovered that this little village didn't possess its own burial place. It was peculiar amongst parishes in that it buried its dead outside its own boundaries. Catherine Anne could not have been buried in the grounds of the Red Chapel, or indeed anywhere else in the village.

I was equally disappointed when I asked about Robert Godfrey Hughes, Catherine Anne's father who was an elder at the church and who had lived in the village some 50 years before. 'Oh yes,' people said. 'If he was a quarry official he would most likely have attended Capel Coch; most of the officials of this period did and many of them were appointed elders.' But there was no chapel or census record of a Robert Godrey Hughes nor Catherine Eluned Hughes, Catherine Anne's mother. The census is held every ten years, so it is possible for people to live in a place, and move away within a census period, without their presence there being officially recorded. But somehow I doubted it in this case.

I came away from Llanberis without even checking to see if its school was a cemented building with a high gable, and whether its teacher had wavy hair and a big moustache and was called Huw Thomas. Quite honestly, I couldn't have cared less. I was fed up with the whole thing. I went home, watched television, and went to bed.

The following day it occurred to me that the hospital might have records. Surely, I said to myself, if a young nurse had walked out of the County Hospital early one morning and committed suicide in an adjoining field by slashing her wrists with a scalpel taken from the hospital, someone inside the hospital would have recorded the fact. So I rang the Records Department of the County Hospital, and the young clerk agreed. She told me there was a sort of hospital log book, very much like a ship's log, and that the matron of the day would record all the hospital happenings in it. She assured me that the suicide of a nurse would certainly warrant an entry, and asked for particulars: the nurse's name, and the date when it occurred.

She rang me back ten minutes later to say that there were detailed records of everything that happened in the hospital from the day it opened to the present time. 'But,' she continued, 'the year 1934 is a complete blank. Not a single word has been written about anything that happened in 1934.' I thanked her for her trouble, feeling rather like John McEnroe at Wimbledon, shaking his racket at the referee and shouting with various blasphemous embellishments, 'I don't believe it!'

I rang Elwyn that evening. I told him of my frustration. I told him the path was there, the stream was exactly where it should be, and the farm Bryn Llwyd Isaf. I told him about the Red Chapel and its three doors and the house with the name Wenfro. I told him that exactly 50 per cent of what we had been told was true, but exactly 50 per cent was downright lies. I was willing to concede that with a bit of extra research, one might perhaps come across Robert Godfrey Hughes, the quarry official and chapel elder. But, whichever way one looked at it, for Catherine Anne Hughes to say she was buried in the grounds of the Red Chapel in Llanberis was a downright lie. 'And surely,' I said, 'real ghosts don't tell lies.'

Elwyn is a cool customer, and his advice was to let it rest for a few weeks and then follow it up. 'You never know,' he said. 'Some more information may come your way in a few weeks' time.'

But I wasn't happy. I was hurt. Somebody had been playing jokes on me and, whoever it was, was a spirit, not a carnal being. I asked Elwyn if he would be prepared to come back to the house again and have another session but he refused. 'If I do come again,' he said, 'I will only be making the same contacts over again. The contacts the other night were extremely strong. I know I will not be able to break new ground in that house.'

The matter was not allowed to rest for long, however. During that week, Heather came to see me and she was worried. She told me how happy they all were after Elwyn and I had called. Overnight, apparently, Catherine Anne had become part of the family in their house. After hearing about her grave, they had decided to visit it the very next Saturday afternoon. It had been a family pilgrimage. They had visited all the churches in Llanberis and then they were directed to the Red Chapel, just as I had been. And, as I did, they also found that there was no grave. They had also asked local people about a fairly large quarry house called Wenfro with a high slate wall around it, but no one knew of such a place. It did not take this little family long to realize that they had also been tricked like me and they were all very hurt. Heather said to me: 'We were all so happy until we went to Llanberis. But we find now that whatever spirit came through to us the other night was nothing but a cheat and a liar.' Then she added: 'We are all now becoming rather fearful for the baby again. A ghost that can lie and cheat us maliciously as ours did is capable of anything.'

There was a new fear in this house, and I felt that Elwyn and I were responsible for it. I felt it was our duty to do something, quite apart from the fact that I was dying of curiosity to know what all this was about. So I phoned him again and this time I asked if he would mind if I asked Winnie Marshall to come and take a fresh look. Elwyn thought this an excellent idea. A fresh medium or sensitive might be able to open new doors. As a research physicist, he also liked things to have tidy endings.

Winnie Marshall is a celebrated medium and healer both in this country and on the Continent. Unlike Elwyn, a scientist who discovered early on that he had a mediumistic gift that he could not understand, Winnie was brought up in the Spiritualist movement. This is her life, and it is a very happy, serene life. She looks through what I might call her 'windscreen' eyes to see ordinary things like the television or how to cross the road but she also has a wide-angled 'rear-mirror' vision, which enables her to see much that is happening in the Other World. She can see what has happened to many of the troubled people who come and see her before they say anything. Somehow or other, she can also see what is going to happen to them. She can see fairly clearly through the veil that separates the Earth from the Spirit world. Sometimes when I think it is unfair that spirits are able to hop in and out of our Earth world while we are prevented from hopping in and out of their Spirit world, I comfort myself with the thought of Winnie Marshall. She is one of us, and yet at times she is able to see them as clearly as they see us. So I asked Winnie if she would come with me to the Eameses' house in Bangor.

I picked her up in Colwyn Bay, but we never mentioned the house we were to visit as we drove to Bangor. We never do. Nor did I say that Elwyn and I had been there before. She knew nothing of Catherine Anne. We all took our places in the same front room again. Winnie requested her special upright chair.

'Well,' said Winnie, without preamble, just as if she was about to remark about the weather, 'you seem to have two very nice old ladies from the spirit world living with you. One of them is very house proud and she is complaining a little about you all – she thinks you are untidy and that you ought to give her a hand with the cleaning. The other lady,' she went on, 'is in her mid-sixties – a very handsome lady, who carries herself well. She has her white hair tied in a tight bun and it is held with a rather unusual red slide that is in the form of a cat.'

'That would be my mother,' said Mrs Eames very quietly.

So we were back to what the family had always imagined the situation to be. They knew about the house-proud ghost, and now Winnie was telling them that Mrs Eames's mother was also living with them. But there was no mention of a nurse, or a suicide, or anyone called Catherine Anne. I had warned them all not to mention to Winnie anything that had gone on before.

Rachel asked Winnie, 'Do you think our two ghosts love our new baby?'

'Your Gran does,' said Winnie. 'She absolutely dotes on her.' And then she added, 'I don't think you need worry too much about the house-proud lady. She looks to me as if she is packing her bags. I don't think she is going to be here long, Something has upset her.'

Then Heather asked, 'Is it our Gran or the other lady who is rocking the cot and going through the drawers at night?'

'It's neither of them, my dear,' said Winnie.' It is a very pretty young lady who is doing that.' She then turned to Rachel. 'Rachel, my dear,' she said, 'did you have an abortion some years ago?'

'Yes, I did,' said Rachel. 'It was about four years ago. It was the doctor – he told me I wouldn't be able to . . .' And then the hanky came out. 'I was bitterly disappointed.' At this the others helped themselves from the tissue box.

'Did you know if your baby was a boy or girl?' asked Winnie.

'No, I didn't know,' said Rachel. 'I never asked.'

'Well I can tell you,' said Winnie. 'She is a little girl and she is so beautiful and she has your eyes and your lovely auburn hair. She is upstairs now, and she has opened the top drawer of the chest that is by the door in the bedroom immediately above us. I think you might have kept baby clothes in that drawer at one time. She has opened the drawer and she is showing me what is inside. I can see three pairs of man's socks rolled up, a biro, a plastic container of cod liver oil capsules and a pair of sunglasses.'

The family looked at her with incredulity but she went on to ask, 'What would you have called your little girl if she had lived, Rachel?' And through a great deal of sniffling Rachel answered, 'Ceri.'

'That's a lovely name,' Winnie said. 'Oh, and she likes it too. She is pointing to herself and smiling. You must all now think of her as Ceri. And if you feel she is present or near to you at any time, you must call her name and speak to her. She is a lovely spirit child and she loves her new little cousin.'

It was the same house, the same family, but a different medium and a very different explanation of the hauntings. Winnie had seen a child of four, who was family. She had seen two elderly ladies, one of whom was the grandmother, also family, and the other was a house-proud lady, not family but a past tenant, who was getting ready to leave anyway. This now was making sense. The previous version of a pregnant nurse who had committed suicide and was connected to some unfamiliar village and a chapel with a strange name, now seemed fictitious and unreal, and just a little unwholesome.

I don't think it occurred to any one of us to speculate which medium was the 'better', which one had got nearer to the truth. I think we all accepted that Elwyn had made real contact. So much of what he told us had later been corroborated and we had all seen the hand of the person telling us the story resting next to his on the arm of his chair. It could be that he had had a crossed line. This sometimes happens on the phone. We pick up the receiver to speak to a friend and we become aware of two other people enjoying a conversation. We know it is a crossed line, we know we should not listen, we should put our phone down, but we seldom do. Perhaps we should have put the phone down on Catherine Anne.

Without saying so in so many words, we all seemed to agree that it was Winnie's message that was the right one for this house. The message about little Ceri, and the explanation that it was she and not some grown woman who had committed suicide who was rocking the cot and unwrapping the tissue parcels made sense to us all. And we felt that it was somehow natural that, if there was a ghost it should be of a member of the family. One could even understand old Elizabeth Edwards, the last tenant, being around.

On the way back to Colwyn Bay, I told Winnie about our previous experience in the house, about Catherine Anne and the Red Chapel. I also told her that I had discovered that half of what we had been told had been true and half false, and that it seemed to me like a scenario that had been planned to turn out this way.

Winnie made no comment. So I tried again. 'Did you see anything of this young nurse tonight?' I asked.

'No', Winnie replied.

'Well, can you explain how it was that Elwyn managed to make such a clear contact with this spirit who called herself Catherine Anne?' I persisted.

Winnie remained quiet for a long time, and I actually thought she had gone to sleep. Then she replied, 'Since you ask, Aelwyn, I think both you and Elwyn were deliberately conned the other night. After all, you did write a book about your ghost experiences, and if I remember correctly, you boasted a little of how you and Elwyn, between you, have a 95 per cent success rate in solving ghost problems. So it is possible that the people of the Spirit World thought it was time to take you down a peg or two.'

'But spirits don't read books, Winnie,' I protested.

'I think they must have read yours, Aelwyn,' she said with a broad smile. 'And it wouldn't surprise me one little bit to know that during the last few days quite a crowd of them from the Summerland have been watching you rushing from Bangor to Llanberis and from one registrar's office to the other, and killing themselves laughing!'

I think she's right. And I think I know who two of them were. It was I who buried one of them, nearly five years ago. It seems that I was the victim of a slightly sick practical joke from the Beyond.

Strangely, when I first toyed with the idea of writing this book, it was this story that was uppermost in my mind. I felt an urge to include it, although I knew very well that it didn't fit into the pattern.

And although my editor suggested it would probably be best placed at the end of the book, it was the first bit that I wrote. I find it most difficult to accept that guides from the Beyond can urge or persuade one to act in a particular way, and yet as far as I can tell, I have only been an agent in the telling of the tale of Catherine Anne. It wasn't me who wrote the story with its 50 per cent fact and 50 per cent fiction. They wrote the plot, and I am becoming convinced that they passed it on to me as a special Plot 7 – and that I have gone and muffed it.

I wonder too if the moral of the story for Earth-dwellers is that those who have gone before us have far more exciting things to do that just lie all day in Abraham's bosom. Perhaps that they want us to know that the people of the Summerland also enjoy a good laugh from time to time.

12   *The White Light*

If I mentioned to the people crouching with me behind the vicarage sofa the idea of passing through a tunnel at death, and of seeing a white light, most of them would know what I would be talking about. Even people who have never read a book in their lives have heard of the tunnel and the white light, but the more knowledgeable would say: 'You are talking about a book by a doctor who interviewed people who had been resuscitated after being pronounced clinically dead, and had asked them to describe what they had seen.'

The book is called *Life After Life*, and it was written by Dr Raymond Moody. I have no idea how many copies were sold but I do know the descriptions of death conveyed in it – passing through a tunnel and seeing a white light – are familiar to millions of people. I remember too how very impressed I was when I read it years ago. It gives such joy and comfort to bereaved families, and indeed to all of us, because one day we will all have to walk through this tunnel. Reading this book should be like reading a travel brochure.

Many people have been brought up without a church background and many who have had such a background no longer attend church. Very often it is not lack of faith but lack of time that keeps people away. But whatever the reason there seems to be a growing proportion of our population going through life without seeing the inside of a Christian church except perhaps for marriages, baptisms and funerals. I have always felt sorry for these non-churchgoers when I have seen them attending the funerals of those who were dear to them. Small families turn up at the crematorium dressed in deep black, and ten of them will huddle together in a pew meant for eight. They keep their heads down and their noses in their tissues, fearful lest the minister should ask them to do or say something. And when they leave at the end, they don't have a clue what it was all about or what was supposed to have happened to the person they all loved so much, or where he was supposed to have gone.

Every crematorium allows a minister a maximum period to carry out the funeral service, usually half an hour, or twenty minutes in busy town establishments. They have to limit the time, otherwise there would be hearse traffic jams on the roads. And half an hour is sufficient time to conduct a funeral service, to give a short tribute and, if necessary, to sing a couple of hymns. But if the mourners have no Sunday school or church background, it is impossible to give instruction in so short a time, or even to begin to tell them what strong evidence there is for believing that their loved one is now free of pain and in a place of great happiness.

Last year I spent a lovely holiday in Bulgaria. I went in the late summer to the mountain village of Borovets, which was built specially for skiers and is 4,000 feet above sea level. It is a most wonderful place. The more I walked in the mountains, the more there was to see. A week, a fortnight, even a month would not have been time enough to explore the wonderful mountains of Borovets. Every morning, as I walked up to the mountain paths I would pass a woman and her five or six children standing under the shelter of a tree. They had six or seven horses of various sizes, and these were for hire. It occurred to me that if only I could ride a horse, I would be able to see more of the beautiful mountains. I also noticed that amongst the horses there was a superior-looking grey mare with a sort of American pommel on her saddle that would make it easier for me to mount. The family didn't seem to be attracting much custom, so I ventured up to the lady and told her, 'I am 76. I have never ridden a horse in my life, but I would love to be able to ride that grey mare over there. Is it possible?' She said to me 'You want me to teach you to ride a horse in one day?'

'Well, in half an hour if you can.'

'I will tell you in five minutes how to ride the grey mare,' she said. 'When you go up mountain you lean forward; when you come down mountain you lean backward.' She also gave me the Bulgarian commands for 'stop' and 'go', and told me the horse's name was April. I paid my money, gripped the pommel, the lady and her children heaved me on to the saddle, and I was away. April and I had a lovely day together after that five-minute 'quickie' on how to ride a horse.

If, however, a family in mourning asked me for a five-minute 'quickie' on the afterlife, they would be asking the impossible – although I did manage it in 90 minutes on one occasion.

A very elderly gypsy matriarch had died and I was to conduct the funeral the next day. She had six middle-aged sons, a number of daughters and more grandchildren than even I had. I called at the eldest son's caravan to arrange the details of the service. As soon as I had stepped over the threshold he said: 'Tell me, Father, what do you think has happened to my mother? Where do you reckon she is at this moment like?'

I began my creed: 'I believe that when a person dies . . .' Before I could go any further, however, the gypsy opened the caravan window, called a little boy and told him: 'Go and find my brothers, lad. Tell them to come here. Tell them the Protestant Father is here with me and he is going to tell us where our mother is now. Hurry, boy!'

Within minutes I had a good congregation of sons, daughters and daughters-in-law waiting quietly for me to begin. They listened, and when I had finished my oration, they shuffled quietly to their feet, mumbled their thanks and left.

It must have been a good sermon, because after the others had gone my host took out his wallet, took every note and every coin out of it, crushed them in his palm and handed them to me. 'To buy flowers for your church,' he said. Back at home, I counted it and it came to £68.73p.

I was glad to have had the chance to talk to them, because gypsies are terrified of death. But it is not possible to say a tenth of what one would want to say in the crematorium's allocated period. Because of this I have always felt desperately sorry for the non-church families who have had to be satisfied with rota parsons at funerals and rationed instruction at crematoriums. It was then that I came across the book *Life After Life*.

The young American doctor who wrote it worked in hospitals at the time when new resuscitation techniques were being tried. He saw the introduction of special teams in every large hospital rushing with trolleys and resuscitation gear whenever the red 'cardiac arrest' button was pressed. Dr Moody began to wonder if some of the people who had been pronounced clinically dead and later brought to life again by these teams had had glimpses of the Beyond in those few minutes they had spent away from their bodies. He asked nearly 200 of them and the replies he received became a talking points almost overnight. Everyone, whether they had read the book or not, somehow came to know about passing through the tunnel and meeting the white light.

I saw in this book a solution to the problem of non-churchgoers. I used my next cremation fee to buy three copies and kept a look-out for the most needy recipients of my newly founded charity. If the mourners knew how to make the sign of the cross, how to say the 'Gloria' and when to stand and when to sit without being told, they were not allocated a free book. I assumed that they would possess at least the few shreds of knowledge a member of the Anglican

Church would have been expected to pick up in a lifetime of church attendance. It was the less knowledgeable families I was looking out for.

When the various undertakers I worked with saw me distributing books to some people and not to others, they became curious. When I explained my purpose to them, they all donated money to buy more books. One book was left in the vestry so that undertakers and cremators could pick it up at odd moments and have a read. The idea was that if there was not a minister around to give comfort, others at the crematorium would be able to shed a little light on the business of dying.

'Well, its like this sir. Take your dear departed mother, sir, God bless her soul. It says in this 'ere book I have read that by now your mum will have passed through the tunnel with the beautiful music, see what I mean, and she would have met the White Light ...'

I carried on presenting books to mourners for some time, until my psychologist daughter Bridget picked one up and read it. She warned me in no uncertain terms to stop giving out this type of book. 'Dad,' she said, 'when certain people read about the tunnel of happiness and the wonderful music, and the meeting with the white light of love, they won't be able to resist it. The coroner will have to have extra staff and you will have more funerals in the week than you will be able to cope with.' She was joking, but in one sense she was right. The book does take away the fear of death, but it also makes it sound just a little bit too exciting – and too pleasant.

Dr Moody was honest enough to say that some of the people he interviewed could remember nothing of what had happened to them. Others who had been resuscitated twice said they had no memory of one occasion but remembered the other vividly.

The doctor describes twelve different symptoms or stages which were described to him. Most of his clients mentioned a few of them, and a good number had experienced six or seven of them. They were:

1   Hearing the voice of the doctor or some other person saying they were dead whilst lying on the bed, or in a place of death;
2   Hearing an uncomfortable noise, or a buzzing, or a ringing;
3   Moving through a dark tunnel, variously described as a cave, a well, a trough, a funnel, a vacuum, a void or a valley;
4   Being outside their body but still in the earth environment;
5   Able to see their discarded body as a strange thing apart;
6   Conscious of being in a new body;
7   Seeing departed family members and friends moving slowly;
8   Experiencing a warm white light coming closer;
9   Having an instantaneous playback of their past life or being encouraged by the white light to recount it;
10   Seeing family and friends more clearly and standing by a fence waving their welcome;
11   Making a conscious decision to return, because they had children to look after, or work to be done, some testifying it was the white light that told them their time had not yet come;
12   A general feeling of absolute peace, tranquillity and joy.

It is the white light that is the main feature of the Afterlife according to these people. It radiates brilliance and perfection and yet it doesn't dazzle; it exudes a warmth of love and joy, peace, contentment and total serenity. Many identified it as Christ Himself. Others said that as it appeared, they felt the need to think loving, compassionate thoughts about others.

I asked some of the ladies behind the sofa with me how many of them could, at the drop of a hat, think loving, charitable thoughts about another. I tell them of a time I had a puncture. A friend of mine who owns a garage stopped his car, came to my rescue and within five minute had the old wheel off and the spare wheel on. It was so easy for him because during his life he had had so much practice. So perhaps the verse from the funeral service that I have treated so lightly is not so stupid after all: 'In the midst of life we are in death.' It suggests that whilst we are still living we should prepare for death, and in this context, we should prepare in particular for our meeting with the white light. If Dr Moody and the people he interviewed are correct, we already know one of the questions we will have to answer in our Summerland Entrance Examination. It is: 'Create in your mind a loving, charitable thought about the person who pinched your lawn-mower last week.'

There are other priceless bits of testimony in Dr Moody's book that corroborate the information I have received over the years from those who have passed away. My ghosts have been at pains to let me know how very difficult it is to communicate in Earth language about Earth times, and Earth numbers and Earth measurements. One of Dr Moody's patients told him the same thing:

> Now there is a real problem for me as I am trying to tell you this, because all the words I know are three-dimensional. As I went through this, I kept thinking, well, when I was doing geometry, they kept telling me there were only three dimensions. But they were wrong – there are more. Of course our world, the one we are living in now, is three-dimensional. But the next one definitely isn't. And that's why it is so difficult to tell you this in words that are three-dimensional. That's as close as I can get to it, but it's not really adequate. I can't really give you a complete picture.

Many people who have had out-of-body experiences have afterwards expressed surprise at the sight of their own body. This too is corroborated:

> Boy, I sure didn't realize I looked like that. You know I am only

used to seeing myself in a picture, or from the front in a mirror, and both of those are flat. But all of a sudden, there was me, or my body, and I could see it, definitely see it, full view, about 5 feet away. It took me a few moments to recognize myself.

One thing that amazed me in the book was Dr Moody's observation of how similar the reports of his different subjects were, even though they came from various religious, social, and educational backgrounds. I wondered if there wasn't something here that also said something about ecumenicalism.

Apart from this, I found little that was new in the book. The yesterday's people I had come across had already been telling me much of what his patients said. I had already heard of the different dimensions and the different timings. I knew about the tunnel, the beautiful music and the white light. It has been whispered to me, but I do not know with how much truth, that some of the more gifted Spiritualist mediums are even able to pick up hearsay information about life in the third and even the fourth existence. It just does not bear thinking about!

I also remember Peter Ramster saying that he had heard of all these things from others. He said: 'The first time I heard of the tunnel and the white light was when my patients, under hypnosis, described them to me as they died in one Earth life before returning to another.' He knew of the tunnel and the white light before he had ever heard of Dr Moody, his patients or his book. But of course, this is just what one would have expected. Dr Moody's information was given to him by people who had not actually completed the crossing, but Peter and I obtained our information from people who had actually died and completely passed over. If Peter's patients could remember several different lives under hypnosis, it was only reasonable that they should also remember a few of their deaths.

Bloxham's patient, Jane Evans, would have had to die as

the wife of a Roman officer, pass through the tunnel, hear the music, meet up with the white light and do all the other death things before she could be born again as Rebecca, the Jewess in York. If she had lived six lives, she would also have experienced six deaths. Yet, to the best of my knowledge, although Bloxham's tapes allegedly reported the rebirth of dozens of his patients, not one of them bothered to tell him what it was like to pass from life to death to life . . .

One of the ladies from behind the sofa has just asked me a very hurtful question. 'All these people Dr Moody interviewed,' she is saying, 'had only been dead a matter of minutes, and yet they said that in that short time they had been able to walk the tunnel, see their relatives, see a flashback of their past and all manner of other things. So,' she asks, 'how is it that you, who have been dead for three days, have seen nothing, and are still hovering around the vicarage staring at your own body?'

My reply is: 'The reason why I am still hovering around, madam, is not, as you suggest, because I am not welcome in the other world, or because my departed family and friends are reluctant to meet me at the fence. It is simply that both Dr Moody's patients and I, after we are dead, will have entered the "eternal present". Only a person of little knowledge would try to compare 15 minutes of Earth time with three days of Earth time within this spiritual state.'

I don't think I have ever questioned the fact of life after death – or least some kind of life after death. But as I grew older I came to learn so much more about this life. I began to write this book in the hope that I might give the same joyful confidence to others that I have always enjoyed myself. I didn't expect that, just by writing, I myself would have my knowledge increased, my faith compounded and the anticipation of dying made more exhilarating. Just as the television commercial tells us it is good to talk, I think it is also good to write. It is always a good thing to put our thoughts, our ideas, our beliefs and our ambitions on paper, even if the paper is only destined for the wastepaper basket at the end of the day.

I have always known that dying doesn't break family ties. In most of the hauntings I have been to, the ghosts we have been called to sort out have been departed members of the family who called us – it is generally *their* grandmother, hardly ever someone else's. But I never did understand why these ties remained so strong after death and how people did not seem to outgrow their roots. My parents have been dead 50 years. During that time I have married and had children, and they in turn have had their own families. I have amassed a number of friends. My parents died without knowing my wife, my children, or most of my present friends. My life is now very different from the one I remember with my parents in Blaenau Ffestiniog. But the ties I feel for them are still strong.

The Bible tells me I will someday depart to a place where there are many dwelling places. Most world religions tells me that at this point I have a choice. There would most certainly be a dwelling place for the famous and the rich. I have added a new word to my vocabulary since I began to write this book: 'gravitate'. I was told that if I wished, I could gravitate towards a dwelling place of my choice on the other side. 'Can I gravitate towards the dwelling place of the famous and the rich?' I asked. And I was told: 'You have a choice; you may gravitate towards any place you wish.' But I have never been rich and I have never been famous. I know already that I would feel uncomfortable and out of place in that particular dwelling place.

I think I have discovered something else about this process of gravitation: that it begins whilst we are still on this earth. I am almost certain that I am waiting here in the vicarage for my grandmother to come and cross me. Recently I have been thinking more and more of my parents and their love. In the same way that a baby turns in the womb as he prepares to begin his Earth experience the old man in the vicarage is beginning to gravitate towards the dwelling place of his parents, Kate and William Lloyd, in the Summerland.

When I was training for the ministry at theological college a wise old parish priest used to come once a term to talk to us. I remember him saying. 'When you put your pen down after finishing writing next Sunday's sermon, ask yourself the question "So what?" I am pleased not to have missed that particular lecture, because it's turned out to contain such invaluable advice. Whether one preaches, writes an article, or gives a talk to the Ladies' Guild, it is always useful to ask oneself, 'So what?' before delivering the message.

I am drawing towards the end of this book, which I consider to be the more mature companion volume to *The Holy Ghostbuster*. It is now time for me to stand back and say, 'So what?' Why did I write the book? What message do I want it to convey? The answer is simple. The message is that over the years I, like my Spiritualist friends, have come to *know* there is life after death. I already possessed this knowledge when I wrote the first book, but my further research into the teachings of other religions, my meetings with more of yesterday's people and my contacts with my friends the Spiritualists have convinced me that not only is there life after death but that it is a happy, beautiful and active life. It is not a place of stupor and eternal rest. There is fun and laughter and meetings with relatives and friends in this Heaven–Paradise–Summerland that we go to after death. Dying is something exciting which is yet to come. So that is the answer to the 'So what?' question: I wrote my books so that I could share my news about the joys of the Afterlife with others.

It is very difficult to look back and assess how successful one's ministry has been over many years, and how much of the joy of the Gospels one has been able to pass on to parishioners. But I did once win a 50p bet with a dying parishioner. I would visit and we would talk quite openly about her impending death. She was a lovely person, but she was an atheist. I would describe to her the wonderful times awaiting her, the music, the tunnel and the white light. She would smile and say, 'I hope you're right but I don't think you are. I believe that when you're dead you're dead and that's the end of it.'

'I'll bet you 50p you're wrong,' I told her.

'Right,' she said. 'You're on, and now I'll go and put the kettle on and make a cup of tea.'

Two weeks later, at the crematorium service, I told her friends that Helen had died owing me 50p and that I was quite sure the determined old atheist had come to realize this by now. When her brother was leaving he pressed a 50p coin into my hand. 'Helen was that honest,' he said. 'She'd be miserable at not being able to pay her debt – especially a gambling debt.'

This book, like my other one, would not be complete if I did not repeat the story of Cis Jones. She was a parishioner of mine, a very shy, private person. She lived like a hermit. I was probably the only person allowed to cross the threshold of her little cottage. Many of the villagers said that she had lots of money, but she lived a very frugal life. She had no relatives or friends, and the only time she left her home was to come to church twice on Sunday. She would be the last to arrive and the first to leave.

In her late sixties she was told by a hospital consultant that she had inoperable cancer, and she was told that she had about six months to live. She was very brave, but she was afraid. Living alone is one thing; dying alone and of cancer is quite another. News of her plight got around the village and women drew up a roster of those willing to help. I am sure the last six months of her life were the happiest Cis Jones had ever experienced. She had never known what it was to give and receive love – but she was a quick learner. There were more peals of laughter coming from her little cottage than from any other house in the village, and it was Cis who was keeping all her carers in stitches. Yet she was in constant pain; her doctor, knowing what was to come, had reserved the morphine for nearer the time when the pain would become intolerable. When this happened he began to prescribe his morphia elixir, but Cis refused to take pain-killers of any kind. She would grit her teeth and groan in pain but she refused to take the doctor's morphia. The doctor told me, and asked if I could persuade her to take his medication. 'Cis,' I said to her, 'the doctor tells me you are refusing to take your medicine. You're very silly – it would relieve you of pain if you took it.' There was no reply, so I tried again. 'Why won't you take it?' It was then she turned and looked at me.

'You're a good one to ask me why,' she said. 'Don't you remember on Easter Sunday two years ago you preached about the resurrection and how we would close our eyes in one world and open them in another, and how we would hear beautiful music and meet the white light of love, and how our parents and loved ones would be standing at the fence waiting for us? You do remember saying all that don't you?'

'Yes,' I said. 'I was quoting Dr Moody and his ...'

But Miss Jones cut me short. 'Well,' she said, 'if all these wonderful things are going to happen to me then why on earth should you think I would be such a fool as to take the doctor's pain-killers and sleeping tablets? When my time comes to go on this wonderful journey I want to be wide awake so that I can enjoy every minute of it.'

Bibliography

Campbell, Eileen and Brennan, J H, *Dictionary of Mind, Body and Spirit*, Aquarian Press, London, 1990

Doctrinal Commission of the General Synod of the Church of England, *The Mystery of Salvation*, Church House Publications, London, 1995

Evans-Wentz, *The Tibetan Book of the Dead*, Oxford University Press, Oxford

Iverson, Jeffrey, *More Lives than One*, Souvenir Press, London, 1976

Moody, Raymond, *Life After Life*, Bantam Press, New York

Muldoon, Sylvan and Carrington, Hereward, *Projection of the Astral Body*, Rider, London, 1929

Ramster, Peter, *The Search for Lives Past*, Somerset Film Company, Sydney, 1990

Rees, Dewi W, 'The Hallucination of Widowhood,' *British Medical Journal*, British Medical Association, London, 1971

'The Hallucinatory Reactions of Bereavement' (MD thesis), University of London, 1971

Zodiac, *Truths Concerning Reincarnation*, Greater World Association